Illustration on the cover is from the title page of the Great Bible, the first authorized English translation (1539). William Tyndale, the pioneer of the English Bible was forced into exile in 1524 and burned as a heretic on October 6, 1536 for translating the Bible into English.

Library of Congress Cataloging in Publication Data

Meherally, Akbarally
Understanding the Bible

ISBN 0-9693571-1-7

Copyright © 1989 Akbarally Meherally
All rights reserved.

A.M. Trust
P.O. Box 82584
Burnaby, B.C.
Canada V5C 5Z1
(604) 298-8803

Typeset by G.T. Laser's Edge Ltd.
Printed in Canada - 1989

> ¶The Byble in
> Englyshe, that is to saye the content of all the holy scrypture, bothe of ye olde and newe testament, truly translated after the veryte of the hebrue and Greke textes, by ye dylygent studye of dyuerse excellent learned men, expert in the forsayde tonges.
>
> ¶Prynted by Rychard Grafton & Edward Whitchurch.
>
> Cum priuilegio ad imprimendum solum.
> 1539.

UNDERSTANDING THE BIBLE

-through Koranic messages-

by
AKBARALLY MEHERALLY

IN THE NAME OF GOD, THE MERCIFUL, THE COMPASSIONATE

> ℭThe Byble in
> Englyhe, that is to saye the content of all the holy scrypture, bothe of ẏ olde and newe testament, truly translated after the verpte of the hebrue and Greke tertes, by ẏ dylygent studye of dyuerse excellent learned men, expert in the forsayde tonges.
>
> ℭPrynted by Rychard Grafton & Edward Whitchurch.
>
> Cum priuilegio ad imprimendum solum.
> 1 5 3 9.

"O God, I acknowledge Thee to be my creator, my governor, and the source of all good things. I thank Thee for all Thy blessings, and especially for letting me practise what I hope is the truest religion. If I am wrong, and if some other religion would be better and more acceptable to Thee, I pray Thee in Thy goodness to let me know it."

Sir Thomas More, *Utopia*, trans. John Dalton (1844). p,128

On the top, King Henry VIII (who had repudiated the authority of Pope) is shown giving copies of the Bible to Archbishop Cranmer and Chancellor Cromwell. In the middle, the Archbishop and Chancellor are shown distributing the copies. At the bottom, the loyal subjects of the King are shown shouting "Vivat Rex." Cover illustration from *Eerdmans' Handbook to the History of Christianity.*

REVIEW

I found Mr. Meherally's book to be a most interesting study and discussion of the early origins of the three principal religions of today.

In my experience, many people form opinions, and have misconceptions, about religions other than their own, based only on assumptions they have made with little or no information. Many Christians, for example, may even assume that Muslims do not worship the same God.

Mr. Meherally's book may be controversial, but it is an enlightening and encouraging work, since it clearly connects all three major religions to the same source – back to Abraham and his family, and to the one Almighty.

The sense of unity thus created narrows the gap between cultures and, if accepted, can greatly ease the conflict in our current world, since so much warfare and bloodshed is based on religious differences and misunderstandings.

I thank Mr. Meherally most sincerely for sharing his knowledge with me, commend him on his efforts and wish his work widespread success.

Stephanie Williamson
Notary Public, Vancouver, B.C.

REVIEW

"As a Christian who has always felt close affinities both with Reform Judaism and with the purest form of Islam, I warmly welcome this controversial little book. Akbarally Meherally is no stranger to controversy. Yet it is never controversy for its own sake but for the sake of truth. There has seldom been a time in human history when there was greater need for open, religious discussion and debate about spiritual things. Never has there been more need for Jews, Christians and Muslims to reexamine their own roots and to trace again the common threads which unite them. They are all children of Abraham, whether physically or spiritually. They are all "people of the book." They are all followers of the one God.

While I do not agree with all of Mr. Meherally's conclusions, I am convinced that Christianity has indeed misunderstood Jesus and that it needs to make a radical rediscovery of his person and message. "Understanding the Bible – through Koranic messages" is a courageous attempt to provoke such a rediscovery, among other things. It is certain to make devout members of all three faiths do some hard thinking. But, this is no bad thing. Jesus himself reminded us that we are to love God "with all our mind!"

I particularly recommend this book to all Jews and Christians who are ignorant of what the Koran has to say about both of their faiths. Meherally says he is not a scholar but he has set forth the relevant passages in a surprisingly scholarly way."

Tom Harpur

Tom Harpur is a nationally syndicated columnist on religion and ethics with "The Sunday Star" and author of the controversial best-seller, "For Christ's Sake." He is a former professor of New Testament at the Toronto School of Theology and was Religion Editor of "The Toronto Star" from 1971 to 1983.

CONTENTS

1. A HEAVENLY THREAD
   'THE PEOPLE OF THE BOOK' 1
   THE MOST WIDELY READ BOOK 3
   WHICH BIBLE? 4
   WHICH KORAN? 6

2. ABRAHAM
   THE PATRIARCH 8
   THE THREE CHILDREN OF ABRAHAM 9
   WHO WAS ABRAHAM? 11
   RECOGNITION OF OTHER SCRIPTURES 12
   SIMILARITIES BETWEEN SCRIPTURES 15

3. ISHMAEL AND ISAAC
   THE SACRIFICE 18
   THE "ADOPTED SON" OR "SEED" 20
   TRIBAL ENVY 21
   THE NUZI LAWS OF MARRIAGE 21
   RUTH AND BOAZ 22
   THE LEVIRATE LAWS 23
   THE SCROLLS FROM THE DEAD SEA 24

4. ABRAHAM AND ISAAC
   TWIN TEXTS 26
   DOMESTIC QUARREL 28
   GOD'S MASTER PLAN 29

5. MOSES
- THE SHEMA 31
- THE BOOK OF MOSES 32
- THE BODY OF A PHARAOH 32
- JEWISH IDOLATRY 35
- THE PROPHECY OF MOSES 36

6. COVENANTS
- THE CHOSEN PEOPLE 38
- THE BIRTHRIGHTS 39
- 'THE CHILDREN OF A PROMISE' 41

7. JESUS
- THE VIRGIN MARY 43
- THE MIRACLES OF JESUS 44
- THE NEW COVENANT 45
- POPE JOHN PAUL 45
- THE 'LAW' 46

8. COUNCILS AND CREEDS
- THE 'TRINITY' 47
- THE EMPEROR CONSTANTINE 48
- THE HOLY SPIRIT 51
- BAPTISM 52
- THE APOSTLE'S CREED 53
- THE ISLAMIC CREED 54

9. TRINITARIANISM
- ANCIENT TRIADS 55
- THE EARLIER REJECTIONS 56
- THE RECENT REJECTIONS 57

10. JOHN
- THE "WORD BECAME FLESH" 59
- FATHER AND SON 61

11. PAUL
- EYEWITNESS TO THE GLORY 64
- THE LIBERTY FROM THE 'LAW' 65
- THE VEIL OF MOSES 66
- THE COVENANT OF CIRCUMCISION 67
- THE CONFLICT OF APOSTLES 69
- 'PAULINE JUSTIFICATION' 70
- THE PROPHECY FOR KEDAR 71

12. PERSONAL SAVIOUR
- BELIEFS IN CHRIST 73
- DEATH THROUGH 'ORIGINAL SIN' 75
- THE SECOND ADAM 76
- ATONEMENT 77
- MERCY AND JUSTICE 79
- AM I CONDEMNED? 80
- MY ABANDONED SAVIOUR 81

13. "THE WAY" NOT "THE DESTINATION"
- Y.H.W.H. 85
- A SECOND OPINION 86
- "I AM THE WAY" 87
- EXPLICIT MESSAGES 88
- "GOD WITH US" 90
- GOD DOES NOT PRAY 90

14. RESURRECTION AND ASCENSION
- THE SACRED 'LIGHT' OF EASTER 92
- THE CRUCIFIED BODY 93
- RESURRECTION 94
- ASCENSION 95

15. MIRACLES
- MIRACLES OF BIBLICAL PROPHETS 97
- MIRACLES OF MUHAMMAD 99
- OTHER MIRACLES 100

16. PROPHECY BY JESUS
- THE "HELPER" 101
- ANOTHER PARACLETE (ANOTHER JESUS) 103

17. REPEATED SUDDEN CREATIONS
- CREATION OR EVOLUTION? 108
- A GREAT DESIGNER 110
- SUDDEN EXTINCTION 111
- SUDDEN ORIGIN OF NEW SPECIES 112

18. COLLECTION OF SCRIPTURES
- THE OLD TESTAMENT 115
- THE NEW TESTAMENT 118
- THE KORAN 119

19. CONCLUSION
- NATIONAL TRADITIONS & CUSTOMS 122
- DO YOU KNOW THIS PREACHER? 128

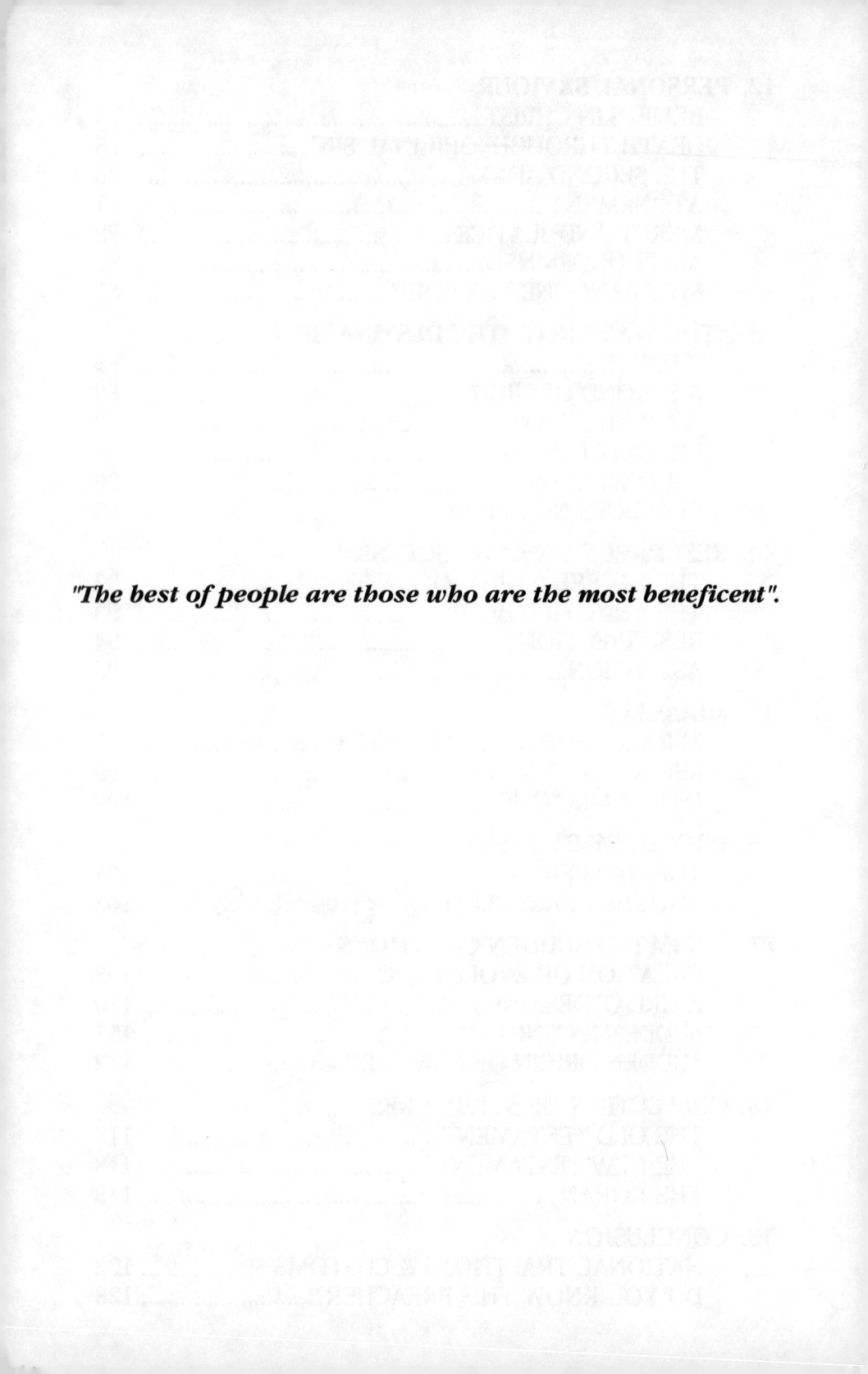

"The best of people are those who are the most beneficent".

1

A HEAVENLY THREAD

> And understand that I am He,
> Before Me there was no God formed,
> And there will be none after Me.
> Isaiah 43:10

'THE PEOPLE OF THE BOOK'

Whenever I have occasion to stay overnight at a motel during a journey across the border, I go through the drawers of the motel furniture and on most occasions find a copy of the Bible, placed by one of the American Bible Societies. Late in the evening I read a few chapters from that Bible to understand the good tidings, the admonitions and the morals that are hidden behind the historical events narrated by the great prophets. Invariably an echo of the words of a Protestant lady editor touches my mind: "A thread is woven through religious history of Judaism, Christianity and Islam."

Today, more than ever before, we find the need for an understanding between these three Children of Abraham. I believe it can be achieved by reading the Bible and understanding the messages of the biblical prophets from a new perspective, a perspective whose outlook is panoramic and vast enough to sweep all three religions. "Judaism, Christianity and Islam are all children born of the same father and reared in the bosom of Abraham," writes professor F. E. Peters.[1] They share not only a common heritage from Abraham but also a common belief in the existence of divine scriptures. The preaching and practices of these religions are based upon the guidance and the norms that are dictated in their Holy Books, the Old Testament, the New Testament and the Koran [2] (Ar. *al-Qur'an*).

If one was to read all the three scriptures, one would immediately notice a continuity of the divine revelations. The Creator has indeed woven a heavenly thread linking these three **Books of Instructions.** The bridges can be built between the **'People of the Books'** if every son and daughter of Abraham reads the books of the other family members and respects their prophets.

In most countries of the world testimonies are affirmed in the Courts by placing a hand on one of the above named scriptures. In other words, the solemnity of one's oath is formally validated by a secular judge when one concedes to bring in the **'Words of God'** as one's witness. This shows that the testifying judge is wordlessly telling the testifier that on the Day of Judgment, the Supreme Judge will judge you - *a man of the book,* by this very *book* upon which you have just placed your hand and taken the oath. In the nineteenth century, an Englishman named Charles Bradlaugh created a commotion when he fought for his right to decline to swear on the Bible. He refused to take a Christian oath to enter the House of Commons after being elected as a member.

---

[1] F. E. Peters, *Children of Abraham* (Princeton: Princeton University Press, 1982), "Preface." Peters was professor of History and Near Eastern Languages and Literature, New York University.

[2] A Muslim would prefer the spelling Qur'an, instead of Koran. Since this book is addressed to non-Muslims as well, I have used the popular Western form 'Koran'.

THE MOST WIDELY READ BOOK

Undoubtedly, the Bible is the most widely read book in the world. Approximately 2.5 billion copies were published between 1815 and 1975, according to the *Guinness Book of World Records*. No other book has been translated into as many languages: Biblical verses can be read in nearly 2000 different tongues. Besides this singular honour, it also has the distinction of being the most controversial piece of writing critically examined, debated, edited, revised and re-revised by monarchs, clergymen, scholars, church-goers and laity alike.

The English word Bible comes from the Medieval Latin/Greek *Biblia* and is derived from a word describing the inner part of a papyrus plant, from which a form of paper was made. Hence, the name simply means 'The Books'. *Bibliotheca Divina* - the Divine Library or Holy Bible, is a collection of sixty-six [3] divine books bound together, 39 of which constitute the Old Testament and 27 the New Testament. These books were written by at least thirty-six authors, all claiming to be inspired by God. The writers were kings, fishermen, farmers, shepherds, ministers, military men, lawyers, priests, a doctor and a tax-collector, and they lived over a period of nearly 1600 years.

The Old Testament was originally composed in Hebrew with some later portions in Aramaic. Hebrew was a language of the Semitic people. There was a period in history when the Christian church did not permit the laity to have access to the Bible. Only the clergy had this privilege. Translation of the Bible into modern languages was expressly forbidden by the Catholic Church. During the early thirteenth century copies of the Bible in the German language were burned by the order of Pope Innocent III. Several owners of the foreign Bible were imprisoned, whipped and sent to the galleys by the Roman Catholic Inquisition.

---

[3] There are seven additional Books of Apocrypha or Deuterocanonical Books that are included in the Roman Catholic canon. Also, there are few Apocryphal Gospels in the New Testament. The Church at large has not accepted them as canonical but scholars study them for comparative studies.

In 1452-5, the first printed Latin Bible, known as the Guthenberg Bible, was printed in Germany. An English Protestant reformer, William Tyndale, made a translation of the New Testament and parts of the Old Testament into English of exceptional literary quality, but he was betrayed and arrested near Brussels in 1535. He was burned as a heretic in October 1536. His last words were reported as, "Lord, open the King of England's eyes." In the 16th century, Martin Luther, the founder of the Protestant denomination and German Reformation, attacked the mediating role of the Church. He began his German translation of the Bible in 1521. The Roman Church was by then compelled to publish its own translations to counteract the Protestant beliefs.

WHICH BIBLE?

I have frequently discussed biblical narrations and texts with Christian scholars and others. Many times, before I finished quoting from one of the books of the Bible, learned opponents of mine stopped me to ask from which Bible I was quoting. Anyone who has not read the different versions of the Bible might find this a strange question. For him any Bible is a Bible. What difference does it make? After reading texts from two different Bibles, one can easily understand why it is important for Christians to know which Bible.

NEW AMERICAN STANDARD BIBLE:

"For there are three that bear witness, the Spirit and the water and the blood; and the three are in agreement." (I John 5:8; text of vs 7 KJV does not appear).

AUTHORIZED KING JAMES VERSION:

"For there are three that bear record in heaven, the Father, the Word, and the Holy Ghost: and these three are one. And there are three that bear witness in earth, the

Spirit, and the water, and the blood: and these three agree in one."(I John 5:7-8)

The words of the added text were injected to the translation by editors, probably in the early fourth century, but they do not appear in the older Greek manuscript. The late Herbert W. Armstrong argued that they were added to the Latin Vulgate edition of the Bible during the heat of the controversy between Rome [4], Dr. Arius [5] and God's People [6].

I wish those who take the liberty of adding words to the scriptures, especially to infer incongruous hypotheses, would read and understand the following verse:

You shall not add to the Word which I am commanding you, nor take away from it...
Deuteronomy 4:2

There are many similar disparities in the various versions of the Bible. In keeping with the above Commandment, I have quoted the biblical texts in this book from the New American Standard Bible, Reference Edition, published by Creation House Inc., of U.S.A. This book, according to its publishers, enjoys universal endorsement as a trustworthy translation of the original text.

In the foreword, the Editorial Board have confirmed that they had "a two-fold purpose in making this translation: to adhere as closely as possible to the original languages of the Holy Scriptures, and to make the translation in a fluent and readable style according to current English usage. (This translation follows the principles used in the American Standard Version 1901, known as the Rock of Biblical Honesty)."

---

[4] The word 'Rome' in this instance, refers to the Roman Empire between 325 and 451 C.E. During this period, Christianity, with its belief of Holy Trinity, was declared as the official religion by Imperial Order.

[5] Dr. Arius (250-336 C.E.) was a senior presbyter and an intelligent scholar. He believed that the Father alone was really God and the Son was different from his Father. He was excommunicated by the Church in 318 C.E., for advocating the 'Unity of God' and opposing the concept of Holy Trinity.

[6] The term 'God's People' refers to the numerous Councils of Bishops held between 325 and 451 C.E.

However, the editorial board also states, "*Italics* are used in the text to indicate words which are not found in the original Hebrew or Greek but implied by it." There are instances where verse after verse has been placed within brackets by various translators themselves, including those of the New American Standard Bible. Twelve verses in the New Testament, starting from John 7:53 to 8:11 can be used as an example. These twelve verses are not found in the most of the old manuscripts. They appear in the later Greek manuscripts and sixth-century codex. It is recorded that over 45 new versions of the New Testament in English were added during this century.

WHICH KORAN?

One may be tempted to ask a similar question of Muslims. Which version of the Koran do Muslims generally believe? Fortunately, there is only one version of the Koran, in Arabic. Professor Arthur J. Arberry [7] writes, "Apart from certain orthographical modifications of the originally somewhat primitive method of writing, intended to render unambiguous and easy the task of reading and recitation, the Koran as printed in the twentieth century is identical with the Koran as authorized by Uthman [8] more than 1,300 years ago." After reviewing so many versions of the previous scriptures, it seems that the Lord decided to guard His final Revelation, the Koran. He so proclaimed and did what He had proclaimed:

> **It is We who have sent down**
> **the Remembrance (the Koran),**
> **and We watch over it.**
> **...and surely it is a book sublime,**

---

[7] Arberry (1905–1969), became professor of Arabic and Head of the Near and Middle East Department at London University in 1946. He was also an immensely prolific and versatile writer on a wide range of topics in Arabic and Persian studies.

[8] The third of the four patriarchal Caliphs of Islam. He died in 35 Hegira/ 656 C.E.

**falsehood comes not to it from before it
nor from behind it...**
Koran 15:9 and 41:42[9]

In this book I have quoted the verses of the Koran from *The Koran Interpreted* by professor Arberry, [10] whose translation is regarded as objective and unbiased. It is composed in a clear and unmannered English, easy to read and understand. Arberry's interpretation, as he prefers to call his translation, is not apt to confuse the reader, because it is written without footnotes or glosses. For the information of my readers, professor Arberry was not a Muslim; his work is purely academic.

Before going on to the next chapter, I wish to clarify that I am not a biblical scholar. I am a research student, with a mind open to suggestions and criticisms. I am placing before you what I have found to be of interest to men of religion and especially to the **'People of the Book'**, that is to say to 16 million Jews, 900 million Muslims and 1600 million Christians.

In the Koran, the term **'People of the Book'** is used for Jews and Christians. However, from an overall perspective, Muslims are also People of the Book, since Islam is founded upon a divinely revealed book - the Koran. In fact, the true Islam acknowledges no other authority than that of the Koran as "the divine authority" and does not acknowledge a hierarchy, such as Papal authority.

---

[9] Numbering of the Koranic verses by professor Arberry differs from the traditional numbering system employed by other Muslim translators. Hence, it is necessary to look a few numbers above or below the number printed to find the exact verse in other translations.

[10] Oxford University Press, paperback edition, 1983.

2
ABRAHAM

**No longer shall your name be called Abram,
But your name shall be Abraham;
For I will make you the father of a multitude of nations.**
                                                  Genesis 17:5

THE PATRIARCH

One day in c.1919 B.C.E., a man who had been known to his tribe for the last 99 years by the name of **Abram** "father of exaltation," was asked by the Lord to change his name to **Abraham** "father of a multitude" *(Peace be upon him)* [11]. Who could have imagined what the Almighty had planned for an old man who had only one son at that age. The Lord alone knew that prophet Abraham would become the father and founder of true monotheism that would encompass more than half the population of this world.

**And He took him (Abraham) outside and said,
"Now look toward the heavens, and count the stars,**

---

[11] In Islam, *'Peace be upon him'* is mentioned after the name of a prophet as an expression of reverence (love and respect, not worship).

> if you are able to count them."
> And He said to him,
> "So shall your descendants be."
>
> Genesis 15:5

Today, the total population of Jews, Christians and Muslims - the three children of Abraham - is 2.5 billion. No one but the Almighty God knows what the count may be in the next century. Will they all be united under one banner and one principle? A principle established by their common patriarch, which expects everyone to submit to **"One God and to Him Alone."**

> Say: "People of the Book!
> Come now to a word common between us and you,
> that we serve none but God,
> and that we associate not aught with Him,
> and do not some of us take others as Lords,
> apart from God."
> And if they turn their backs,
> say: "Bear witness that we are Muslims."
>
> Koran 3:56

THE THREE CHILDREN OF ABRAHAM

Ishmael, the eldest son of Abraham *(Peace be upon him)* was born when his father was 86 years old. Before his birth, the angel of God said to his mother, **"You shall call his name Ishmael** (meaning, *God shall hear*), **because the Lord has given heed to your affliction."** (Genesis 16:11). Ishmael fathered **"...twelve princes according to their tribes."** (Gen. 25:16). The Bible has recorded the names of these twelve princes and mentioned that they settled from Havilah to Shur, which is east of Egypt and towards Assyria. According to Arab genealogists, Ishmael was the progenitor of the Northern Arabs, the Mustariba (i.e. Aramite tribes) which were assimilated among the Arab-Muslims. After the death of Sarah, Abraham married Keturah and had six more sons from whom issued among others the South Arabian tribes of Sheba and Dedan.

Ishmael married a daughter of Jorhamite prince named Mudad and she gave him an illustrious son named Kedar (Ar. *Qaidar*). In the Bible, there is an important prophecy about a descendant of Kedar which we shall observe in the latter part of this book. Kedar was an ancestor of Adnan (or *Qais*), who was progenitor of the tribes of Northern Arabia and forbearer of the prophet Muhammad *(Peace be upon him)*.

The Arabs are essentially an Ishmaelite race!

Isaac, the second son of Abraham *(Peace be upon him)*, was born fourteen years after the birth of Ishmael. Isaac was the ancestor of the 'House of Israel', the 'House of Judah', as well as of Jesus, the son of Mary *(Peace be upon him)*. One night, Jacob, the son of Isaac *(Peace be upon him)* wrestled with an angel of God until daybreak and would not let his opponent go unless he would bless him. So the angel said to Jacob, **"Your name shall no longer be Jacob, but Israel; for you have striven with God and with men and have prevailed."** (Gen. 32:24-28). The angel had to physically dislocate the socket of Jacob's thigh to win. **"Therefore, to this day, the sons of Israel do not eat the sinew of the hip which is on the socket of the thigh..."** (Gen. 32:32).

The Arabs and the Israelites are cousins!

Before the birth of Ishmael, the angel of the Lord had said to his mother, **"I will greatly multiply your descendants so that they shall be too many to count...his hand (will be) against everyone, and everyone's hand (will be) against him; and he will dwell (live) before the face of (to the east of) all his brothers."** (Gen. 16:10-12). It can be said that what we are watching in the Middle East today was predestined or predicted 4000 years ago, before the birth of Ishmael and Isaac. Are we merely the pawns? Or, was the outcome of our free-will foretold in the Bible? In the next chapter we shall be reviewing more on the subject of tribal envy between the descendants of Ishmael and Isaac.

WHO WAS ABRAHAM?

Abraham (Ar. *Ibrahim*), was the tenth generation from Noah *(Peace be upon him)*. He was a Hebrew, a term that comes from Eber or Heber, the great-great-grandson of Noah. Abraham was a native of the Chaldean and came from the city of Ur in the biblical land of Shinar, near the junction of two rivers, the Euphrates and the Tigris. In those days, Ur was a great metropolis and cultural centre. Some of the world's most influential cultures flourished on the banks of these two rivers: the Sumerian, Assyrian and Babylonian. Professor Jacob M. Myers writes, "Abraham was thus far from being a half-civilized nomad subject to the whims and fancies of those among whom he moved. He was a wise, shrewd, powerful caravan trader, carrying on his business at every important trading post in the land."

In the Hebrew Scripture, the first occurrence of the word "Prophet" refers to Abraham. Abraham allowed no idolatry in his household. Allah [12] gave him the singular honour of *Khalillullah* (friend of Allah). The Koran tells us, **"And God took Abraham for a friend."** (4:124). He was *Hanif* (adherent to immutable Monotheism). **"...and when it had become clear to him that his father (Azar) was an enemy of God, he (Abraham) declared himself quit of him..."** (9:115).

When Abraham came to Canaan [13] from the place of his birth, God promised him:

...Now lift up your eyes
and look from the place where you are,
northward and southward and eastward and westward;
for all the land which you see,
I will give it to you and to your descendants forever.

---

[12] The word Allah is a contraction of *al-ilah*. The definite article *"Al"* (meaning "the") joined with *"ilah"* (Divinity). Literally, *Allah* means 'The God' or 'God'. The term is not subject to gender or plurality. Every time a Muslim uses the word Allah, he is reminded of the "The One and Only God."

[13] The extent of Canaan is described in Genesis 10:19 as being from Sidon to Gaza.

> And I will make your descendants as
> the dust of the earth;
> so that if anyone can number the dust of the earth,
> then your descendants can also be numbered.
>
> Genesis 13:14-17

The "promised land" was given by God, **"to you and to your descendants forever,"** meaning, to all the three descendants of Abraham - Jews, Christians and Muslims. If the promised land and the prophecy attached to it was meant for the House of Israel alone, then God would not have said **"I will make your descendants as the dust of the earth (countless)."** Jews number only sixteen million, whereas there are over 2.4 billion Christians and Muslims.

Often we hear that Abraham was Jewish, a term applied to the tribe of Judah (colloquial *Jew*). Judah was the great grandson of Abraham; hence he cannot be called a Jew. He cannot be called an Israelite, meaning a descendant of his own grandson named Jacob *(Israel)*. He was an ancestor of Jesus Christ but obviously not a follower of Christ. His religious beliefs were not founded upon the Torah or the Bible, because he lived over three centuries before Moses *(Peace be upon him)*, the "law-giver."

The Book of Genesis tells us that Abraham died at the age of 175 and was buried by his sons Ishmael and Isaac in a tomb in the cave of Machphelah, in the modern town of Hebron. Arabs call the town *al-Khalil* (the friend), and the Mosque in Hebron is known as *al-Haram al-Ibrahimi* (the Sanctuary of Abraham).

RECOGNITION OF OTHER SCRIPTURES

It may sound new to many non-Muslims that the Koran not only acknowledges the previous messages revealed to the major biblical prophets but also directs every Muslim to affirm the Book of Moses (Ar. *Tawrat*), the Songs of David (Ar. *Zabur*) and the Gospels of Jesus (Ar. *Injil*) as heavenly books. Islam goes beyond and recognizes the religion established by Abraham - the great patriarch of all monotheistic religions. However, it does not endorse the messages that have been revised or edited later.

In the Koran, there are narrations and accounts of Aaron, Abraham, Adam, Alexander, David, Elijah, Elisha, Enoch, Ezekiel, Ezra, Isaac, Ishmael, Jacob, Jesus, Jethro, Job, John the Baptist, Jonah, Joseph, Lot, Mary, Moses, Noah, Saul, Solomon, Zachariah and others.

Christianity also acknowledges the messages that arrived prior to the ministry of Jesus but it falls short of endorsing the messages that came after, although there are premonitions of the future revelations in the Gospel of John, which we shall observe in the later chapter.

During his ministry as a master teacher, Jesus often quoted from the Old Testament. On his final day, Jesus called upon his heavenly Father from the Cross, reciting the Psalms: *"Eli, Eli, lama sabachtani?"* that is to say, **"My God, my God, why hast Thou forsaken me?"** (Psalms 22:1).

Judaism accepts only the Hebrew Bible as a divine scripture. In the Jewish canon, traditionally fixed at the Synod of Jabneh about C.E. 100, the books are divided into three parts: 'the Law' (*Torah* - the Pentateuch), 'the Prophets' (*Nebi'im* - the prophetic writings) and 'the Writings' (*Ketubim* - the Psalms, Proverbs etc.). They accept a total of thirty-nine books in their canon. Jews do not recognize any revelations subsequent to their own. Hence, they do not acknowledge the New Testament or the Koran as divine scriptures. Neither do Jews recognize the prophets that came subsequent to theirs, although there are premonitions of such arrivals in the Fifth Book of Moses. We shall review that prophecy in the later part of this book.

It is not uncommon to find a copy of the Bible in a Muslim home. A follower of Islam would read the previous scriptures with a new vision, a perception that has been widened, as well as enlightened, by a later scripture - the Koran. Commentators of the Holy Koran have often compared the Biblical narrations with the Koranic revelations to show how, and to what extent, human intervention can exaggerate or alter the portrayal of an event that did take place in history.

As an example; I quote below two versions of the catastrophic destruction caused by an overwhelming flood (deluge) in the days of prophet Noah.

THE BIBLICAL VERSION:

**The water prevailed fifteen cubits (270 inches) higher,
and the mountains were covered.
And all flesh that moved on the earth perished,
birds and cattle and beasts and
every swarming thing that swarms upon the earth,
and all mankind; of all that was on the dry land,
all in whose nostrils was the breath of
the spirit of life died.
Thus, He blotted out every living thing
that was upon the face of land, from man to animals,
to creeping things and to birds of the sky,
and they were blotted out from the earth;
and only Noah was left,
together with those that were with him in the ark.**

Genesis 7:20-23

THE KORANIC VERSION:

**But they (Noah's people) cried him (Noah) lies;
so We delivered him,
and those with him, in the Ark,
and We appointed them as viceroys,
and We drowned those who cried lies to Our signs;
then behold how was the end of them
that were warned!**

Koran 10:74

The first description speaks of **the entire mankind,** beasts and birds, upon the earth being blotted out. The latter speaks of **the tribe of Noah** - who rejected the Signs - being overwhelmed in the flood.

According to the Bible, Noah's flood occurred in 2370 B.C.E. This was the Pyramid Period of the Old Kingdom in Egypt. The power of Pharaoh was at its height. The Egyptians had built the second and the third Pyramids of Giza. The period of the 3rd to the 6th dynasties (c.2614 - c.2181 B.C.E.) is pre-eminently the time when the royal pyramid in stone was the chief monument left by each successive king. There is no record of the total destruction of the Egyptian civilization. The dynasty continued and the names of the kings are recorded by Egyptologists.

I remind my readers that I am merely trying to pinpoint the end result of repeated human elaboration on an inspired text. To say that the original message or the inspired communique erred would be to disown the scripture itself - a sacrilege and an irreverence. All I try to convey is that statements can become exaggerated or understated, depending upon the limitations of comprehension or the practices of the person editing and updating a document. Many of the original texts of the Bible, written by inspired saintly persons, were destroyed after revisions. Later on, the revised texts were repeatedly rectified and updated by various interested groups to accommodate their own points of view. The important question is, were these editors and re-writers divinely inspired or were they merely hired or decreed by secular and/or religious hierarchies?

SIMILARITIES BETWEEN SCRIPTURES

The question is often asked, Is there a similarity in texts between the Bible and the Koran? The answer is Yes and No. The Koran is not a copy of the Bible, but it includes stories of the biblical era narrated in the Bible, as well as others that are not in the Bible. Of course, historical events and names remain unchanged, but the text is not identical. Similarly, the Koran speaks of the traditions and beliefs of Jews and Christians but does not correspond to the modified versions of their creeds and annals.

Just as the New Testament cannot stand alone without the Old Testament, the Koran cannot teach Islam without narrating the accounts of the past and the moral lessons behind them. If it had left out the glorious act of Creation and the history of mankind from that day onwards, especially the events connected with the previous messengers, then the 'Revelations of God' - the Koran, would have been an incomplete document. It would not have been possible to expound the Islamic points of view and to explain how, where and why they differ from the traditional beliefs of the past. In fact, you would not have been reading this book, because I would have had no base upon which to make this comparative study.

The religious instructions that are imparted in both the Bible and the Koran are conveyed by the same **Instructor,** so there must be a similarity in the fundamental instructions. But the Koran goes beyond and examines the previous instructions.

There are several interesting stories of the biblical prophets in the Koran which do not appear in the Bible. Below is one such anecdote from the life of the prophet Abraham.

> One day Abraham went to the temple of his father and **"he broke them (idols) into fragments, all but a great one."** He then placed the device of demolition (sword or staff) beside the chief idol. When the people noticed what had happened to their gods (idols) they suspected Abraham and said to him: **"So, art thou the man who did this unto our gods, Abraham?"** Abraham replied: **"No; it was this great one of them that did it. Question them (idols), if they are able to speak!"** The people, including the father of Abraham; **"...were utterly put to confusion saying, 'Very well indeed thou knowest these do not speak."** Abraham immediately retorted by questioning the rationality for worshipping idols instead of Allah, which speak not and added, **"that which profits you nothing, neither hurts you?"** Abraham concluded by saying: **"Fie upon you and**

that you serve apart from God! Do you not understand?" (21:59-69).

> Say: "We believe in God,
> and that which has been sent down on us,
> and sent down on Abraham and Ishmael,
> Isaac and Jacob, and the Tribes,
> and that which was given to Moses and Jesus, and the Prophets, of their Lord;
> we make no division between any of them,
> and to Him we surrender."
>
> Koran 3:79

3
ISHMAEL AND ISAAC

> Do not urge me to leave you
> or turn back from following you;
> for where you go, I will go,
> and where you lodge, I will lodge.
> Your people shall be my people,
> and your God, my God.
>
> Ruth 1:16

Ishmael (Ar. *Ismail*), the eldest son of Abraham, was born when his father was 86 years old. Fourteen years later, Isaac (Ar. *Ishaq*) was born. (Gen.16:16 and 21:5).

THE SACRIFICE

Ishmael, the first-born son, has not been given the glory of being the **"eldest son."** He has been systematically and deliberately deprived of the honour and glory due to him for being offered as a sacrifice by his father.

ISHMAEL AND ISAAC

God decided to test the faith of Abraham and said:

> **Take now your son, your only son,
> whom you love,_____,
> and go to the land of Moriah;
> and offer him there as a burnt offering
> on one of the mountains of which I will tell you.**
> Genesis 22:2

The important question is who was this **"only son"** of Abraham that was offered for sacrifice? Ishmael the eldest son or Isaac the second son? The Bible writers have placed the name of Isaac in the blank space above. Muslims believe Ishmael was the one that was taken by Abraham for the sacrificial offering. Every year, Muslims throughout the world celebrate *Id al-Adha* as a day of festivity, recalling the courage and patience of Ishmael and the unwavering devotion of Abraham.

Note: The word **"only"** is very significant. In the Hebrew text the word used is ***yachid*** and not *echad*, which identifies the absolute singularity - the one and only one.

The Bible story continues further. After the sacrificial offering (in which God provides a ram to replace the son of Abraham), the Lord says:

> **...since you have not withheld your son,
> your only son, from Me.**
> Genesis 22:12

In both the above quotations the Lord uses the word **"your only son."** Obviously, the logical answer is that the incident must have taken place before the birth of Isaac, the second son of Abraham. So, what could be the reason that the name of Isaac appears in the blank space, as the **"only son"** of Abraham? Bible scholars explain that anomaly by putting forward the following arguments.

After the birth of Isaac, Ishmael lost his status of being a son of Abraham, since he was not born of a wife of Abraham but born to a handmaid of Abraham's wife. According to Jews and Christians, the Lord had recognized Isaac, the one that was born to the wife of Abraham, as the **"only son"** of Abraham.

The biblical passage below tells us that Ishmael never lost his status as a **"son,"** not even after the birth of Isaac. If Ishmael had lost the status, the Lord would not have used the word **"sons"** in the following verse.

> **Then his sons Isaac and Ishmael,**
> **buried him (Abraham)**
> **in the cave of Machpelah...**
> Genesis 25:9

THE "ADOPTED SON" OR "SEED"

Another explanation put forward by Jews and Christians is based upon cuneiform tablets found from the library of King Ashurbanipal (669-627 B.C.E.). On these tablets are the writings which exemplify the law of the 2nd and 3rd millennium B.C.E. regarding *adoption*. This law states that a childless man would adopt a son to serve him in his old age. Should a son be born later to the man, the adopted son's status as an heir would be altered.

This is not a valid argument with respect to Ishmael, since *Ishmael was not an adopted son.* He was fathered by Abraham.

A further argument that I have often heard is that because Ishmael was born to a handmaid and not to a wife of Abraham, he would qualify as a **seed** or a **descendant** of Abraham, but not as a **son**.

This argument is nullified by the following:

1. Prevailing Nuzi Laws of marriage, referred to later in this book, tell us that such marriage contracts were legal in the days of Abraham and the child born of a handmaid would have the same status as one born to the wife, even if the wife had a child of her own later.

2. There is a very similar incident in the Bible, of Ruth and Boaz, where a child born to a slave girl is recognized as a son. The details are provided in the following pages.

TRIBAL ENVY

So, is it out of tribal rivalry that the descendants of Isaac *(Jews)* are concealing these facts and depriving the preeminence due to the descendants of Ishmael *(Arabs)*? In *Encyclopaedia Judaica Jerusalem, volume 9*, under the heading "Ishmael" it is written:

> It is related that a renowned traditionalist of Jewish origin, from Qurayza tribe and another Jewish scholar who converted to Islam, told Caliph Omar ibn 'Abd al-'Aziz (717-20) that the Jews were well informed that Ismail (Ishmael) was the one who was bound [14], but they concealed this out of jealousy.

THE NUZI LAWS OF MARRIAGE

Jacob M. Myers of Gettysburg, Pennsylvania has been a professor at the Lutheran Theological Seminary and a contributor to *Interpreter's Dictionary of the Bible*. He is recognized as a leading expert on the Old Testament. In his book *Invitation to The Old Testament* [15] he writes:

> Archaeological discoveries help us to fill in the details of the biblical narrative and to explain many of the otherwise obscure references and strange customs that were commonplace in Abraham's world and time...... A Nuzi marriage contract provides that a childless wife may take a woman of the country and marry her to her husband to obtain progeny.

---

[14] Bound by Abraham before the sacrifice.

[15] Doubleday & Co., Inc., New York (1966) page 26.

But she may not drive out the offspring even if she later has children of her own. The child born of the handmaid has the same status as the one born to the wife. That is why, when Sarah wanted to drive out Hagar and Ishmael, it was quite objectionable to Abraham - because of the legal custom of the region from which he came, he was reluctant to do so. It required a special divine dispensation to act contrary to that custom. **"And God said to Abraham, 'Do not be disturbed over the lad and your handmaid. Listen to Sarah and do everything she tells you..."** (Gen. 21:12-13).

The above quoted Nuzi Law of marriage establishes the fact that a child born of a handmaid to a childless father has the same status as one born to his wife and cannot be treated differently, even after the birth of a child to his wife.

RUTH AND BOAZ

In the Old Testament [16], there is a fascinating story describing in detail the vivid circumstances under which Boaz, a landowner of Bethlehem, meets a slave girl named Ruth and marries her. Ruth was a young widow and a slave girl. Her mother-in-law, Naomi wanted a **"resting place"** for her daughter-in-law so she instructed Ruth:

> **Wash yourself therefore, and anoint yourself and put on your best clothes, and go down to the threshing floor; but do not make yourself known to the man until he has finished eating and drinking. And it shall be when he lies down, that you shall notice the place where he lies, and you shall go and uncover his feet and lie down; then he will**

---

[16] The Book of Ruth, Chapter 3 and 4.

> tell you what you shall do. And she said to her, "All that you say I will do." So she went down to the threshing floor and did according to all that her mother-in-law had commanded her. When Boaz had eaten and drunk and his heart was merry, he went to lie down at the end of the heap of grain; and she came secretly, and uncovered his feet and lay down. And it happened in the middle of the night that the man was startled and bent forward; and behold, a woman was lying at his feet. And he said, "Who are you?" And she answered, "I am Ruth your maid. So spread your covering over your maid, for you are a close relative."

Thereafter, Boaz redeemed his maid Ruth and married her. She gave birth to a son named Obed. Later on, Obed - the son of a maid - became the founder of the royal line of Israel, an ancestor of both king David and of the great prophet Jesus. If a son of a widowed Moabitess [17] slave girl could have the honour of being the progenitor and forbearer of the most important lines of descent for both Jews and Christians, then why cannot Ishmael - a son of an Egyptian handmaid, be offered by his father for a burnt offering as his "only son"?

THE LEVIRATE LAWS

One may be inclined to argue that the deceased husband of Ruth was a **"close relative"** of Boaz and as such under the Levirate Laws marriage to a widow of a close relative was an acceptable custom. Whereas, Hagar was not a close relative of Abraham.

This reasoning is void since Levirate Laws came into existence much later. Secondly, the close relationship was

---

[17] Moabite and Midianite women were used to lure Israelite males into immorality and idolatry of Baal. Ammonite and Moabite were not allowed to enter the assembly of the Lord for ten generations.

claimed by Ruth but it was denied by Boaz. Boaz was not the closest kinsman (relative) of Elimelech, the father-in-law of Ruth. The Bible confirms this fact and records that the closest relative of Ruth said to Boaz: **"Buy it for yourself"** and so Boaz **"Bought (Ruth) from the hand of Naomi."**

THE SCROLLS FROM THE DEAD SEA

When the new texts were made, the older texts of the Torah were destroyed by the Hebrews. In 1947, some Bedouin shepherd boys of the Taamirah tribe were smuggling goats into Palestine and were passing through the cliffs of Qumran. As luck would have it, one of the goats strayed and one of the shepherd boys threw a stone into one of the caves on the cliff above, idling or perhaps to bring out the strayed goat. He heard the sound of something breaking or his stone hitting a big clay pot. Inside the cave, the shepherd boys found tall jars filled with bundles of manuscripts. They had found the safeguarded copies of the destroyed manuscripts of the Torah as well as some other apocryphal books and documents belonging to a group of monks known as Essenes. These sacred scriptures were hidden by the monks to protect them from the Roman army, which was destroying the Jewish culture. These manuscripts were written on scrolls and were discovered in various caves located in the cliff in the vicinity of the Dead Sea. Hence, they are known as the Dead Sea Scrolls.

Between 1947 and 1954, many more of these ancient scrolls were discovered from Qumran Wadi Murabbat and Khirbet Mird. These scrolls take us back to the original Massoretic Text. Most of the scrolls have been purchased by, or are in the possession of Jewish Universities, institutions and merchants. In 1956 the Hebrew University and Magnus Press, Jerusalem, published a few columns from the Scrolls discovered from *Cave One*. These published columns give us a detailed account of Abram and Sarai being driven by famine to Egypt and Pharaoh taking away Sarai for her beauty. The story does not continue further to the incident of the sacrifice by Abraham of his "only son."

In 1968, the texts recovered from *Cave Four* were published by J. M. Allegro in *Discoveries in the Judaean Desert*. These texts also appeared in *Journal of Jewish Studies 23 (1972)*. Here again, the text comes close to the incident that happened at the land of Moriah but does not continue further. It is often mentioned that some of these discovered scrolls are in such a delicate and fragile condition that they cannot be unrolled any further. I am not aware of any published text from the Dead Sea Scrolls that includes the narration of the sacrifice. But, that does not necessarily mean that I have read all the published texts. I would be obliged if such a text could be brought to my attention.

The question is, if the name of Ishmael was to appear in one of the scrolls as the one offered for sacrifice by his father, then would the Jews and Christians be willing to sacrifice their pride and replace the name of Isaac in their scriptures?

4
ABRAHAM AND ISAAC

> A people who continually provoke Me to My face.....
> who eat swine's flesh.
> And the broth of unclean meat is in their pots.
> Isaiah 65:3-4

TWIN TEXTS

In the previous chapter we saw the controversy concerning the names of Ishmael and Isaac. There are similar controversies concerning the names of Abraham and Isaac. After reading the following twin narrations, it may be speculated that the scribe(s) who wrote the texts may have repeated the events and replaced the name of Abraham with Isaac in the repeated narrations.

TWIN TEXT NUMBER ONE

A   Abraham's wife Sarah was a very beautiful woman. Abraham travelled to Gerar (a town in Southern Israel). The town was ruled by King Abimelech. The Bible says: **"And Abra-**

ham said of Sarah his wife, "She is my sister." So Abimelech King of Gerar sent and took Sarah. But God came to Abimelech in a dream of the night, and said to him, **"Behold, you are a dead man because of the woman whom you have taken, for she is married." "Then Abimelech called Abraham and said to him, "What have you done to us?"** (Genesis 20:2-9).

B   Isaac's wife Rebekah was a very beautiful woman. Isaac goes to Gerar. The town was ruled by King Abimelech. The Bible says: **"When the men of the place asked about his wife, he said, 'She is my sister,' for he was afraid to say, 'my wife,' (thinking) the men of the place might kill me on account of Rebekah, for she is beautiful." "Then Abimelech called Isaac and said, 'Behold, certainly she is your wife!' How then did you say, 'She is my sister?"** (Genesis 26:7-10).

TWIN TEXT NUMBER TWO

A   Servants of King Abimelech had seized Abraham's well of water. Abraham complained of it to the King. The Bible tells us **"And Abimelech said, 'I do not know who has done this thing...' And Abraham took sheep and oxen, and gave them to Abimelech; and the two of them made a covenant... And he (Abraham) said, 'You shall take these seven ewe lambs from my hand in order that it may be a witness to me, that I dug this well'. Therefore he called that place Beersheba[18]; because there the two of them took an oath."** (Genesis 21:25-31).

B   The Bible tells us: Isaac goes to Beersheba

---

[18] The word *Sheba* (or *Shibah*) means seven. Beersheba refers to the well of oath of a covenant by seven (ewe lambs).

and **"he built an altar there, and called upon the name of the Lord, and pitched his tent there; and there Isaac's servants dug a well. Then Abimelech came to him from Gerar..."** The King made a covenant with Isaac. **"So he (Isaac) called it Shibah; therefore the name of the city is Beersheba to this day."** (Genesis 26:23-33).

Notes:

1. In the gazetteer of places for the biblical lands, there is only one city that is named Beersheba.

2. The opening sentence says that Isaac **"goes to Beersheba"** and pitches his tent there. This shows that a city named Beersheba existed before his arrival in the city.

3. When Isaac was a child of the age of weaning, **"Abraham made a great feast on the day that Isaac was weaned."** Sarah - the mother of Isaac, saw Ishmael mocking at the weaning child of her. So she said to Abraham: **"Drive out this maid (Hagar) and her son..."** So Abraham sent Hagar and her boy Ishmael away. **"And she departed and wandered about in the wilderness of Beersheba."** (Genesis 21:8-14). This story from the Bible tell us that a place called Beersheba existed when Isaac was only a weaning child.

DOMESTIC QUARREL

The above paragraph *(Note # 3)* tells us that it was a family quarrel in Abraham's household that separated the two branches of Abraham. The effects of that domestic rivalry on the issue of rights and precedence are being felt to this day. The time gap of nearly forty centuries has not subdued the feelings. The spirit of envy and rivalry has turned into more serious hatred. The obsession of Sarah to **"drive out Hagar and her son"** has been transmitted from generation to generation. Had Sarah been flexible and yielding, the course of history would have been different. There is one more incident that we find in the biblical history that has widened the gap between the descendants of Ishmael and Isaac.

Ishmael's daughter Mahalath *(Bashemath)* was married to Isaac's son Esau, who is also called Edom. Esau and Jacob were twin brothers. One day Jacob, whose name was latter on changed to Israel, disguised himself as Esau upon the advice of his mother and tricked his father (who was blind due to age) into bestowing upon him the legal birthright of his elder brother Esau. (Genesis 27:5-29). Because of this treachery, Jacob *(Israel)* earned the unrelenting anger of Esau *(Edom)*. Many of these Edomites married the descendants of Ishmael. Some of them live in the Hashemite Kingdom of Jordan and Palestine. And many of them are bitter foes of the children of Jacob, to this day.

GOD'S MASTER PLAN

When Sarah told Abraham to drive out Hagar and her son Ishmael, Abraham was greatly distressed. He was not prepared to separate his eldest son from the family. **"But God said to Abraham, 'Do not be distressed because of the lad and your maid; whatever Sarah tells you, listen to her..."** (Genesis 21:12). Thus, Abraham was led by God into separating his two sons.

If Ishmael and his mother had not migrated to Beersheba and from there to the wilderness of Paran *(Arabia)*, then the descendants of Ishmael could have, most probably, followed the same religious course as did Jews and Christians.

When God separated the two branches of Abraham, He made a promise to Abraham: **"And of the son of the maid I will make a nation also, because he is your descendant."** (Genesis 21:13).

Could it have been God's plan that when one branch of Abraham deviates from the fundamental principles of True

Monotheism and repeatedly transgresses the covenants, then He could teach all over again the principles established by Abraham through a new messenger, to the separated other branch and fulfil His promise of making another nation **"also,"** out of it?

> ℭThe Byble in
> Englyshe, that is to saye the content of all the holy scrypture, bothe of ý olde and newe testament, truly translated after the veryte of the hebrue and Greke textes, by ý dylygent studye of dyuerse excellent learned men, expert in the forsayde tonges.
>
> ⓟrynted by Rychard Grafton & Edward Whitchurch.
>
> Cum priuilegio ad imprimendum solum.
> 1 5 3 9.

5
MOSES

> Let my teaching drop as the rain,
> my speech distill as the dew,
> as the droplets on the fresh grass
> and as the showers on the herb.
> *(Song of Moses)* Deut. 32:2

THE SHEMA

Nearly two and a half centuries after the death of Abraham a "divinely beautiful" child was born in a Hebrew family in Egypt. The ruling Pharaoh's decree was to kill every male child born to a Hebrew mother. But this "man of the God" was not only spared by a Divine Decree but raised as a member of the Pharaoh's household by Pharaoh's own daughter.

Moses led the Israelites out of Egypt to Sinai and out of the tyranny of the Pharaoh. With his persistent efforts, he formed a centre of consolidation for the early Semite tribes. The acceptance of Yahweh as God by these tribes, rather than their ancestry, made them a community of Jews. Moses is considered to be a patriarch of Jews. He taught them the credo of their religion, the great Shema:

Hear, O Israel: The Lord our God is one Lord.

THE BOOK OF MOSES

The Bible records that Moses brought with him Ten Commandments inscribed on two tablets of stone from Mount Sinai. The Koran acknowledges, **"Yet before it (Koran) was the Book of Moses for a model and a mercy."** (46:12).

The Bible records, **"...God called to him from the midst of the bush, and said, 'Moses, Moses!"** (Exodus 3:4). The Koran also verifies that God spoke with Moses from behind a burning bush. He is therefore referred to as *Musa Kalimullah* meaning **Moses who spoke with God.**

The tradition has ascribed, and it is yet believed by many, that the first five books of the Old Testament (known as Books of Moses), were written by the prophet Moses. But that is not totally correct. In the Fifth Book of Moses, Chapter 34 Verses 7 and 8, we read:

**Although Moses was one hundred and twenty years old when he died, his eye was not dim,
nor his vigour abated.
So the sons of Israel wept for Moses
in the plains of Moab thirty days;
then the days of weeping *and* mourning for Moses
came to an end.**

Obviously, Moses could not have written, what happened, thirty days after his death.

THE BODY OF A PHARAOH

The deliverance of the people of Israel from the bondage of the Egyptian Pharaohs by crossing the Red Sea and the journey of Moses and his people from Egypt to the wilderness of Sinai are vividly described in the Second Book of Moses, entitled "Exodus." The parting of the Red Sea by a miracle is one of the illustrious stories of the Bible. Some biblical scholars have argued that the Hebrew word *yam suph*, literally means "sea of reeds or rushes or bulrushes" and hence Moses and his people could have crossed a swampy area and not the Gulf of Suez, known as the arm of the Red Sea.

Others have argued that Pharaoh and his army could not have been **"swallowed up"** by the **"surging waters"** which **"proceeded to cover them,"** if it was crossing a mere marsh land. The Bible tells us:

> **And the waters returned and covered
> the chariots and the horsemen,
> even Pharaoh's entire army
> that had gone into the sea after them;
> not even one of them remained.
> But the sons of Israel walked on dry land
> through the midst of sea...**
> Exodus 14:28-29

The Koranic revelations do not mention the name of the sea that Moses crossed, but it speaks of **a prophecy** about the body of Pharaoh that was swallowed up by the parted sea.

> **And We brought the Children of Israel over the sea;
> and Pharaoh and his hosts followed them
> insolently and impetuously till,
> when the drowning overtook him,
> he (Pharaoh) said, "I believe that there is no god but He
> in whom the Children of Israel believe;
> I am of those that surrender."
> "Now? and before thou didst rebel,
> being of those that did corruption.
> So today We shall deliver thee with thy body,
> that thou mayest be a sign to those after thee.
> Surely many men are heedless of Our signs."**
> Koran 10:90-91

In 1898, nearly thirteen centuries after the revelation of the above verses, the body of Pharaoh of the Exodus was discovered by Loret at Thebes in the King's Valley. The body has since then been moved to Cairo. Mr. Maurice Bucaille, an author, after examining the mummified body, writes in his book *The Bible, The Qur'an and Science* [19], under a Chapter entitled "The Exodus":

> Elliot Smith removed its (body's) wrappings on the 8th of July, 1907: he gives a detailed description of this operation and the examination of the body in his book *The Royal Mummies (1912)*. At that time the mummy was in a satisfactory state of preservation, in spite of deterioration in several parts. Since then, the mummy has been on show to visitors at the Cairo Museum, with his head and neck uncovered and the rest of body concealed under a cloth.

At the end of the chapter, Mr.Bucaille writes an interesting note:

> It is always desirable for man to apply himself to the preservation of relics of his history, but here we have something which goes beyond that: it is the material presence of the mummified body of the man who knew Moses, resisted his pleas, pursued him as he took flight, lost his life in the process. His earthly remains were saved by the Will of God from destruction to become a sign to man, as it is written in the Qur'an.
>
> Those who seek among modern data for proof of the veracity of the Holy Scriptures will find a magnificent illustration of the verse of the Qur'an dealing with the Pharaoh's body by visiting the Royal Mummies Room of the Egyptian Museum, Cairo!

---

[19] American Trust Publications, Indianapolis, Indiana, (1978).

JEWISH IDOLATRY

The Old Testament and history confirm that although the Shema was on the lips of every Jew and also on their door posts, the children of Israel had not accepted the message of Shema with their hearts. The most important Commandment of their Lord was: **"You shall have no other gods before Me."**

While Moses was on the mountain for forty days and nights the Israelites became impatient, and led by Samiri, made a statue of a golden calf. They worshipped it, sacrificed to it, and bowed before it. They ate, drank and revelled in song and dance around the calf, which represented God.

The Bible records that after the passing away of Moses, Jews continued to offer sacrifices to Baal [20] and other heavenly hosts, of which they had learned from the Egyptians, the Babylonians, and the Canaanite tribes. In 2 Kings, Chapter 22 it is mentioned that the copies of the 'Law' were kept secret and hidden. When a copy of 'Law' was discovered, during repairs to a damaged house of the Lord, it was read in the presence of King Josiah (reigned from 659-c.to 629 B.C.E.). After hearing the 'Law' the King realized **"our fathers have not listened to the words of this book, to do according to all that is written concerning us."** He became so upset that he **"tore (his) clothes...and wept before Me (God)."** He burned down the wooden chariots of the Sun-god and the vessels made for Baal that were kept in the Synagogues by the Jewish high priests.

Idolatry among Jews had become so prevalent that they had **"...built the high places of Baal to burn their sons in the fire as burnt offering to Baal."** (Jeremiah 19:5). History has recorded that as early as the sixth century C.E., the chosen people of God, had pictures of the Sun-god and other heavenly bodies in their Synagogues. One such pictorial design appears in *A History of Judaism* [21], under chapter "Judaism and Islam." Inscription below the design reads, "The large, central medallion of the mosaic floor from Bet Alpha Synagogue

---

[20] A Canaanite god. The terms is also applied to the false god.

[21] Daniel Jeremy Silver, (New York: Basic Books Inc.)

(sixth century C.E.). Helios driving the horses of the sun is shown in the centre, surrounded by the twelve signs of the Zodiac, with Hebrew-Aramaic identifications. The four seasons are pictured in the corners."

After the advent of Islam, the children of Israel noticed that the high arches, walls and domes of the Islamic Mosques were all decorated with beautiful floral designs, intricate geometrical patterns and above all with the Koranic verses in artistic calligraphy. Mr.Silver writes, "In this environment Jews felt compelled to apply the second commandment with rigor. The mosaic floors of Palestinian synagogues, with their florilegium, legendary animals, and zodiac circles, were covered up. No painter of the seventh century would have dared to duplicate the frescoes of the synagogue of Dura-Europos. New synagogues were bare of design except for intricate biblical texts in stucco or low relief proclaiming God's oneness and promise." (*A History of Judaism*, page 323).

THE PROPHECY OF MOSES

As observed earlier, the mission of the prophet Moses for establishing the "Unity of God" was not completed during his lifetime. There was a need for another prophet or prophets to complete the mission. The spiritual development of mankind has been gradual and in stages. The Lord prophesied through Moses:

> **I will raise up a prophet
> from among their countrymen* like you,
> and I will put My words in his mouth,
> and he shall speak to them all that I command him.**
> Deuteronomy 18:18

Note: * In the margin of the above translation, it is written that the word '**countrymen**' is Lit.,'***brothers***'. Hence the second line would translate; **"from among the brothers (brother tribe) of yours."**

Christians claim that Jesus Christ was the prophet that was predicted by Moses. Muslims claim the prophecy applies to prophet Muhammad[22] who was raised **"from among the brother tribe of Moses"** and he was the one from whose mouth came the Revelations of God (**"My words"**). Muhammad spoke **"to them all that I (God) commanded him."**

As for the Jews, they were looking for the prophesied prophet when they asked John the Baptist, **"Are you Elijah?"** - **"Are you the Prophet?"** (John 1:21). Maybe one day the Jewish community will recognize someone **"from among their brothers"** as their prophesied prophet.

Then sent We Our Messengers successively, whenever its Messenger came to a nation they cried him lies...

Ah, woe for those servants! Never comes to them a Messenger, but they mock at him.

Koran 23:46; 36:29

---

[22] Born in about the year 570 C.E.

6
COVENANTS

> If his (David's) sons forsake My law,
> and do not walk in My judgments.
> If they violate My statutes,
> and do not keep My commandments,
> Then I will visit their transgression with the rod,
> and their iniquity with stripes.
>
> Psalm 89:30

THE CHOSEN PEOPLE

One day I was looking for the word 'covenant' in *The New Webster's Dictionary of the English Language.* Under 'covenant (Bible)' the definition read, **"the agreement between God and his chosen people, the Israelites."** I then picked up the Bible and discovered that the first covenant God made was with Noah (Gen. 6:18). The second covenant God made was with Noah and his descendants and every living creature of the earth (Gen. 9:9). Thereafter God made several covenants with Abraham and his two sons. And finally I came to the covenant made by God with the Israelites through the prophet

Moses. Once again I was seeing the familiar pattern of glorifying the twelve tribes of Israel as "His" people and overlooking the others.

In the Hebrew language, the word 'covenant' is the same that would be used for an international treaty. Often we find in the political history of the Jewish people that they would contend one of God's covenants in the same manner as a political treaty. From a Koranic point of view all such covenants are in fact declarations from Allah. They are not agreements or treaties between two parties of equal status. It is God that takes the initiative of His own free will and choice, draws up the terms and then declares them or reveals them to His servants. The Koran has also defined such covenants by using such terms as "We bestowed favours" or "We Blessed." The believers can only enjoy these covenants or favours of God as long as they continue to abide by the commandments of God and do not transgress the covenants.

> **What shall I do with you, O Ephraim? (son of Joseph);**
> **What shall I do with you, O Judah? (son of Jacob).**
> **For your loyalty is like a morning cloud,**
> **And like the dew which goes away early...**
>
> **For I delight in loyalty rather than sacrifice,**
> **And in the knowledge of God**
> **rather than burnt offerings.**
> **But like Adam they have transgressed the covenant;**
> **There they have dealt treacherously against Me.**
> Hosea 6:4; 6:6-7

THE BIRTHRIGHTS

Bene Yisrael meaning the Children of Israel - Israelites - have been proud in asserting their birthright as the result of a covenant concluded between their God Yahweh and His people. They claim a kind of monopoly on the phrase "our God" of their Shema, which says: **"Hear O Israel; The Lord our God is one Lord."**

Anyone born of Jewish parents is considered by Jews to be a chosen person in the eyes of God, and all others are not.

During the crisis in Ethiopia, the orthodox Jews did not accept the Ethiopian Jews who migrated to Israel as their own people because they were not from the same stock and had not been converted to Judaism by Orthodox rabbis. Recently, in July 1989, the Israeli Supreme Court defined "who is a Jew" in landmark decision. Under the new rulings, the Israeli Government is asked to accept all branches of Judaism, including Reform and Conservative congregations. Persons converted to Judaism by non-Orthodox rabbis have the right to come to Israel as Jews.

The following narrations from the Old Testament, the New Testament and the Koran show that it is erroneous to consider oneself as a chosen person in the eyes of God by reason of birth alone.

1. In the opening chapter of the Book of Malachi, the Lord declares; **"Yet I have loved Jacob; but I have hated Esau."** Jacob and Esau were twin brothers born to Rebekah, the wife of Isaac. In fact, Jacob was so named because he **"came forth (at birth) with his hand holding on to Esau's heel."** (Gen. 25:26). This proves that God's promise of "chosen people" did not make both the sons of Isaac (twin brothers) "chosen." One was loved, while the other was hated.

2. One day Jesus said to the Jews **"...and the truth shall make you free."** The opponents of Jesus Christ began asserting their birthright and said, **"We are Abraham's offspring."** Jesus was quick to point out, **"...everyone who commits sin is a slave of sin...If you are Abraham's children, do the deeds of Abraham."** (John 8:32-39).

3. The Koran records:

**Say the Jews and Christians,
"We are the sons of God, and His beloved ones"
Say: "Why then does He chastise you for your sins?
No; you are mortals, of His creating;**

> He forgives whom He will,
> and He chastises whom He will."
>
> Koran 5:21

'THE CHILDREN OF A PROMISE'

Ecclesia, the Great Christian Church believes that Christians are **'the children of a promise'**. After quoting the above mentioned example of the "twin brothers" (Esau and Jacob), the apostle Paul writes:

> ...it is not the children of the flesh
> who are children of God,
> but the children of the promise
> are regarded as descendants.
>
> Roman 9:8

Paul, who was known for his inhospitable feelings toward the Jewish people and their traditions, holds that Jews are the Children of Abraham by flesh, whereas, Christians are the Children of God by a **"promise,"** through one particular **"seed"** of Abraham (Jesus).

This notion comes from God's promise to Abraham:

> "And in your seed all the nations of the earth
> shall be blessed."

In his Epistle to Galatians (3:14-16), Paul contends that the said promise was a spiritual promise of *grace.* It was not in your seeds (plural) but in your seed (singular), and **"that is, Christ."**

If this argument is to be admitted and the belief associated with it to be affirmed as truth, then there is one important issue to be recognised. The said promise of blessing or grace **"in your seed"** appears in Genesis 22:18. It was made to Abraham **"in the mount of the Lord"**, when he had obeyed the command of his Lord, completed the ceremony of the sacrifice of his **"only son"**, and was about to return home with Ishmael. The said verse in its entirety reads: **"And in your seed all the nations of the earth shall be blessed, because you have obeyed My voice."**

Consequently, the said promise would relate to the seed of Ishmael who was living with Abraham at that time and was a partner in the ceremony of the sacrifice, in the mount of the Lord. Isaac was not yet in the picture. He was born years later.

The prophet Muhammad was a **"seed"** of Ishmael. He received the "Revelations of God" **(Koran)** which is delivered to **"all the nations of the earth"** and the Koran has made Islam **"a nation also."** (Gen.21:13). Hence, it can be said with a confidence that the Lord has fulfilled the two-fold nature of His promise to Abraham, through prophet Muhammad and Islam.

> **We have not sent thee (Muhammad),**
> **save as a mercy unto all beings.**
> **And We send down, of the Koran,**
> **that which is a healing and a mercy...**
> Koran 21:107 and 17:84

Note: When the issue is of the *sacrifice*, Christian scholars argue that Ishmael was **"a seed"** and Isaac was **"a son"** of Abraham. When the issue is of *grace*, Isaac is recognized as **"a seed"** of Abraham and Ishmael is bypassed.

> **The Byble in**
> Englyshe, that is to saye the content of all the holy scrypture, bothe of ye olde and newe testament, truly translated after the veryte of the hebrue and Grrke tertes, by ye dylygent studye of dyuerse excellent learned men, expert in the forsayde tonges.
>
> Prynted by Rychard Grafton & Edward Whitchurch.
>
> Cum priuilegio ad imprimendum solum.
> 1 5 3 9.

7
JESUS

> When the angels said,
> "Mary, God gives thee good tidings of a Word from Him whose name is Messiah, Jesus, son of Mary;
> high honoured shall he be in this world and the next, near stationed to God."
>
> Koran 3:40

THE VIRGIN MARY

Whenever I have divulged the fact that the Koran confirms the birth of Jesus through the Virgin Mary most of the believers of Jesus Christ with whom I have talked have been taken by surprise. Continuing a little further, I reveal to them that the Koran explains, **"Truly, the likeness of Jesus, in God's sight, is as Adam's likeness."** (3:52). If Allah could create Adam without both the parents, it is easy for him to create with one parent.

Prophet Jesus holds an exalted place in Islam. Here are some of the names and titles mentioned in the Koran for Jesus:

ruhun mina' Llah	("Spirit from God")
kalimatu-Llah	("Word of God")
as-saalihiin	(the righteous)
masih	(Messiah)
nabi	(Prophet)
rasul	(Messenger of God)
Isa ibn Maryam	(Jesus, son of Mary)

THE MIRACLES OF JESUS

Finally, when I disclose that the Koran acknowledges most of the miracles performed by Jesus, the listener invariably wants to know more about the Koranic views on his Crucifixion, his Resurrection, the doctrine of Holy Trinity, etc. It is all in the Koran. This is not a book for Muslims alone; it is for all mankind.

> When God said, "Jesus Son of Mary,
> remember My blessing upon thee
> and upon thy mother,
> when I confirmed thee with the Holy Spirit,
> to speak to men in the cradle, and of age;
> and when I taught thee the Book,
> the Wisdom, the Torah, the Gospel;
> and when thou createst out of clay, by My leave,
> as the likeness of a bird, and thou breathest into it,
> and it is a bird, by My leave;
> and thou healest the blind and the leper by My leave,
> and thou bringest the dead forth by My leave..."
>
> Koran 5:109-112

The Koran tells us that every miracle performed by Jesus was by **"My leave."** The New Testament also confirms that it was the power not of Jesus, but of God that performed all these wonders: **"Jesus the Nazarene, a man attested to you by God with miracles and wonders and signs which God performed through him in your midst"** (Acts 2:22). Jesus acknowledged that fact when he said, **"...but the Father abiding in me does His works."** (John 14:10).

THE NEW COVENANT

Five hundred years before the birth of Jesus Christ, a prophet named Jeremiah predicted:

> **"Behold, days are coming," declares the Lord, "when I will make a new covenant with the house of Israel and with the house of Judah, not like the covenant which I made with their fathers in the day I took them by the hand to bring them out of the land of Egypt, My covenant which they broke, although I was a husband to them," declares the Lord.**
>
> **"But this is the covenant which I will make with the house of Israel after those days," declares the Lord, "I will put My law within them, and on their heart I will write it; and I will be their God, and they shall be My people."**

Jeremiah 31:31-33

From the above we understand:

1. The children of Israel and Judah had broken the covenant, although God was a husband to them.

2. The Lord will now place His 'Law'[23] within **"the People of a New covenant,"** and they will be **"the People of God."**

POPE JOHN PAUL

In August 1989, at his weekly general audience at the Vatican. Pope John Paul implied that the Jewish covenant with God had been broken and superseded by the Christian covenant. *Reuter News Service* reported that the Pope told several thousand pilgrims that God had created **"a New covenant"** with his people through Christ, because of "Is-

---

[23] In the Hebrew Scripture the word 'Law' refers to Torah; related to the verb Hohrah, meaning "to instruct in, to teach."

rael's infidelity to its God." The Pope made his comment first in Italian and then in English.

This infuriated the 'Chosen People', the people of the original covenant. *The Anti-Defamation League of B'nai B'rith,* a U.S.-based Jewish organization, condemned the view expressed by Pope Paul as prejudicial to Jews and asked the Vatican to make an "urgent clarification."

THE 'LAW'

Christians claim that they are the people of the "New-Covenant," and have taken the place of Jews as "His people." With this honour comes added responsibilities and obligations. The responsibility that the Lord had placed upon the **'People of the New Covenant'** was of keeping the 'Law' in their hearts. The following story tells us which is the foremost lesson that one should discern from the 'Law'.

One day, a man well versed in the 'Law' *(a scribe)* asked Jesus Christ, **"What commandment is the foremost of all?"**

Jesus answered:

> **The foremost is, "Hear, O Israel; The Lord our God is One Lord; and you shall love the Lord your God with all your heart, and with all your soul, and with all your mind, and with all your strength."**

And the scribe said to Jesus:

> **Right, Teacher, You have truly stated that He is One; and there is no one else, besides Him.**
>
> Mark 12:28-32

If the **'People of the New Covenant'** were to study the 'Law' **"with all your mind"** and not with borrowed mind, then they would be able to understand the foremost message of their beloved Jesus, **"You shall love the Lord your God with 'all' your heart and 'all' your soul."** A love that is not shared by another person or 'Persons'.

8
COUNCILS AND CREEDS

> Do not think that I came
> to abolish the Law or the Prophets,
> I did not come to abolish, but to fulfil.
> Matthew 5:17

THE 'TRINITY'

The Trinity is a Christian doctrine of God as three 'Persons', equally God. Ask a Christian do you worship three gods. And the answer you get is No. There are three 'Persons' but the Godhead of the Father, of the Son, and of the Holy Spirit, is One; such is the Father, such is the Son, and such is the Holy Spirit; the Glory equal, the Majesty co-eternal, neither compounding the 'Persons' nor dividing the Substance.

The origin of this doctrine can be traced to ancient religions that existed long before Christianity. Please try to imagine in the back of your mind:

1. There are three faces. One is facing you, the second is facing left and the third is facing right. The three faces are of the same size but are placed on a single head.

2. There are three faces. All three are facing you. One is in the middle and the other two are on the right and left of the centre face. They too are of the same size and placed on a single head.

A Christian may say that is an image from the books of Greek mythologies or from an artifact from ancient Egypt or India. Resentfully he would say, Trinity is not a pagan theory. In the Christian doctrine of Trinity there is only One Father not three Fathers, One Son not three Sons, and One Spirit not three Holy Spirits. And none is greater than the other or before or after the other in time; hence the glory is of One that is co-equal and co-existent.

How did this doctrine, foreign to the Old Testament, enter traditional Christianity? The **'Law'**, the keeping of which was made incumbent upon the **"People of the New Covenant,"** had all along promoted pure and simple monotheism. The prophets of the Old Testament had advocated belief in One Almighty God, which was easy to understand and explain. The God of Noah, Abraham, Isaac, David, Moses and even of Jesus was not so confused. They all spoke of a single entity that was jealous and would resent the idea of sharing His Glory with anyone else. What was wrong with that monotheism? Even after a period of one and half millennium, the Christian Church has not been able to come out with an explanation that is easy to understand or could justify the necessity for having a triune of 'Persons' and then unify them as co-equal and co-eternal.

**- - for you shall not worship any other god,
for the Lord, whose name is Jealous, is a jealous God.**
Exodus 34:14

THE EMPEROR CONSTANTINE

The theory of Trinity and its implied renunciation of the biblical teachings of monotheism, developed over several centuries and through many controversies. When the Church-advocated doctrine of Trinity was made the **law of the land** by Constantine, it became an integral part of Christian beliefs. The scholars who wanted Christianity to be based upon the **'Law of the Lord'** *(the Torah)*, were banished and excommunicated by the Church.

David F. Write, Senior Lecturer in Ecclesiastical History at the University of Edinburgh, has written a detailed account of the development of the doctrine of the Trinity and the Christology in one of the several handbooks published by Eerdmans.[24] Below is an excerpt:

> Arius was a senior presbyter in charge of Baucalis, one of the twelve 'parishes' of Alexandria. He was a persuasive preacher, with a following of clergy and ascetics, and even circulated his teaching in popular verse and songs.
>
> Around 318 C.E., he clashed with Bishop Alexander. Arius claimed that Father alone was really God; the Son was essentially different from his Father. He did not possess by nature or right any of the divine qualities of immortality, sovereignty, perfect wisdom, goodness and purity. He did not exist before he was begotten by the Father. The Father produced him as a creature. Yet as the creator of the rest of creation, the Son existed 'apart from time before all things'. Nevertheless, he did not share in the being of God the Father and did not know him perfectly.

In 325 C.E., the Emperor Constantine was faced with two serious controversies that divided his Christian subjects - the observance of true Christian passover on Easter Sunday, and the concept of Trinity which was being challenged by Arius and others.

The Emperor called the *Council of Nicaea* to settle these controversies. Support for the Arianism was growing. The new territories of Constantine were split over a "theological trifle" according to Mr. Wright. The Council met in the Impe-

---

[24] *Eerdman's Handbook to The History of Christianity* (Herts, England: Lion Publishing, Berkhamsted and Grand Rapids, Michigan: Wm. B. Eerdman's Publishing Co.), Chapter, "Councils and Creed."

rial Palace under the Imperial auspices. The Council of priests approved the observance of Easter Sunday and the doctrine of *homoousious* meaning, of co-equality, co-eternity and consubstantiality of the second person of the Trinity with the Father. The Doctrine became known as the "Creed of Nicaea." Arius was quickly condemned and later excommunicated. In 335 he was readmitted to the Church but in the following year he died before his reinstatement.

As a political and civil ruler, Constantine made it an Imperial Law to abide by the Council's decision. Constantine was a pagan ruler. To him it mattered little if such a doctrine contradicted the basic principle of a monotheistic religion or negated the fundamental command pronounced by the Old Testament. Constantine was declared "baptized" on his death bed when water was poured on his forehead in 337. The years of hard labour and the sufferings of scores of prophets for the last two thousand years or more were sacrificed by one Royal Decree. The Sword of Constantine could make it a law to confess the Creed of Nicaea (the Trinity), as the Christian doctrine, but it could not penetrate the human brain and slaughter the confusion the Creed had created.

The words of the Creed, "God from God, Light from Light, True God from True God," do not resolve the problem of expressing Lord Jesus Christ, the Son of God, from the substance of the Father, the one Almighty maker of all things visible and invisible, as True God. Jesus as truly man and yet as truly God. How could one person be both a truly Creator and a truly created?

After the death of Arius, the first Christian Roman Emperor - the Great Constantine, died. His successor Emperor Constantius supported Arianism. In 359, the Arian definition was accepted for the entire Roman Church. Constantine's nephew Julian had the throne from 361 to 363. He rejected the faith of his uncle and tried to revive the worshipping of pagan gods. He was called "Apostate" because of his hatred for Christian beliefs. Thereafter, in 451 C.E., the Emperor Theodosius made a law by Imperial Decree that required all people to accept the Nicene Creed - a modified version of the Creed of Nicaea - as an accepted Christian theology. This modified doctrine of Trinity was approved by the Council of Chalcedony. The Chalcedonian definition said, "...the human nature and the divine nature are unmixed, unchanged, undivided..." Often scholars have used the term "Christ of Chalcedony" for Jesus. The Trinity Document has survived since then and so has the confusion created by the Councils.

THE HOLY SPIRIT

St. Augustine taught that the Spirit proceeded not from the Father alone but also from the Son. The Greek theologians believed that the Spirit proceeds from the Father through the Son; this is called 'double procession'. It found its way into the Nicene Creed by the addition of the word *'Filioque'* (Latin, "and the Son").

To comprehend the doctrine of Christian Trinity requires a mind that can harbour self-contradictory perceptions and yet solicit harmony and tranquillity. It is easy to conclude the Father and the Son as two distinct 'Persons', but it is difficult to conclude that the Spirit is also a 'Person' like the other two. The Greek word *pneu'ma*, meaning **"spirit,"** comes from *pne'o*, meaning to breathe or blow . This word is in neuter gender. In the King James Version of the Bible, the word translated appears as "the Spirit **itself**" (Roman 8/16 and 26).

Christianity professes that the Holy Spirit emanates from God and yet is God. The Koran teaches that Allah is self-sufficient, self-existing and totally independent. God does not emanate from any other source. From a simple and rational point of view, anything that is issued from, or emanates and comes from a source without *(not within)*, cannot be recognised as a primary source but a secondary source. Hence, the Holy Spirit that has emanated cannot be the same as its source.

If someone argues and says that the Holy Spirit is same as its source then what he is saying is that there was total emanation or 100% transfer. If that be the case, then the primary source has either annihilated itself (or Himself) or has reproduced a clone.

To all such logical arguments and apprehensions the parting remark that one may hear from a preacher or an advocate of the Holy Trinity could be, "He who would try to understand the mystery fully will lose his mind. But he who would deny the Trinity will lose his soul."

Here are the responses to such a remark:

> **...do not despise prophetic utterances.**
> **But examine everything carefully,**
> **hold fast to that which is good...**
>
> **You shall love the Lord...with all your mind.**
>
> 1 Thessalonians 5:20-21; Mark 12:30

BAPTISM

> **Go therefore and make disciples of all the nations,**
> **baptizing them in the name of**
> **the Father and the Son and the Holy Spirit.**
>
> Matthew 28:19

Often this particular verse is quoted to support the Nicene Creed of Trinity. It is argued that Jesus himself had said to baptize all the nations in the name of the Father, the Son and the Holy Spirit, and thus the doctrine of Trinity stands endorsed by the Scripture and the Christ.

Of course, the ceremony of Baptism does mention the three names and in the same sequence and order as the Trinity, but the most important factor is **the status.** Where does it say that the three identities are co-equal? It could very well be a sequence for religious hierarchy in faith. In the political arena there could be similar sequence of command, for example; An Emperor, his Minister and his Military Commander. But, the Emperor and his appointee - the Minister, are not equal. The Minister, by the virtue of being so opted, has a better status than the rest of the subjects. He can be considered as a chosen citizen and be so honoured. But, the Emperor would not condone his subjects if they were to call or glorify the chosen citizen as Emperor.

Tom Harpur, former religion editor of the Toronto Star,

writes in his recent publication *For Christ's Sake* [25], "All but the most conservative of scholars agree that at least the latter part of this command(Matt. 28:19) was inserted later."

THE APOSTLE'S CREED

The undermentioned text from *Eerdman's Handbook to The History of Christianity* tells us that until the early third century C.E., the 'Three' were separate and each had his or its own status.

> Hippolytus's [26] account of baptism at Rome at the outset of the third century is very important: 'When the person being baptized goes down into the water, he who baptizes him, putting his hand on him, shall say: "Do you believe in God, the Father Almighty?" And the person being baptized shall say: "I believe." Then holding his hand on his head, he shall baptize him once. And then he shall say: "Do you believe in Christ Jesus, the Son of God, who was born by the Holy Spirit of the Virgin Mary, and was crucified under Pontius Pilate, and was dead and buried, and rose again the third day, alive from the dead, and ascended into heaven, and sat at the right hand of the Father, and will come to judge the living and the dead?" And when he says: "I believe," he is baptized again. And again he shall say: "Do you believe in the Holy Spirit, in the holy church, and the resurrection of the body?" The person being baptized shall say: "I believe," and then he is baptized a third time.

Hippolytus's **Old Roman Creed**, seen above, is the earliest close parallel to the well known **Apostles' Creed.** In the Apostles' Creed the words **"Jesus is our Lord"** are added to the Old Roman Creed.

---

[25] Oxford University Press, Toronto. (1986). p.84.

[26] Died about 235 C.E.

A legend may tell you that the Apostle's Creed was jointly composed by the Twelve Apostles, each one contributed a clause, but the Creed has no direct link with the Apostles. The earliest text dates from about C.E. 400.

THE ISLAMIC CREED

In Islam, the affirmation of Creed is fundamental. It is known as *Shahadah* (to testify). It is regarded as the first and foremost of the 'Five Pillars of Islam'. A person has to recite and affirm the following two statements (just ten words in Arabic) to become a Muslim. There is no immersion in water (physical or symbolic). The text of the Islamic *Shahadah* (Creed) reads:

> ***Ashhadu al-la ilaha illa-Llah, wa,***
> ***ashhadu anna Muhammadar-rasulu-Llah.***

Which translates:

> **I perceive (and bear witness) that there is no god except The God, and, I perceive (and bear witness) that Muhammad is the Messenger of God.**

Two statements united as One text for *Shahadah*. But these two identities are never united as One. The latter is considered the chosen servant of the former.

In 2 Corinthians 13:14 (in some version verse 13) it says:

> **The grace of the Lord Jesus Christ,**
> **and the love of God,**
> **and the fellowship of the Holy Spirit...**

Here again, the three names are mentioned but they are not shown as co-equal or "3 in 1."

> **Say: "Praise belongs to God,**
> **and peace be on His servants whom He has chosen."**
> **What, is God better, or that they associate?** [27]
> Koran 27:60

---

[27] A Muslim takes pride in the language of the Koran. The above verse precisely and beautifully explains the concept in three simple sentences. In the Arabic text, there are three rhythmic words in these three lines.

9
TRINITARIANISM

**Fourth century Trinitarianism
was a deviation from the early Christian teachings.**
The Encyclopedia

ANCIENT TRIADS

From the Near East to the Far East, long before Christianity, mankind used to believe in various triads of God. It is difficult to ascertain who initiated Trinitarianism. However, the concept of a triune God was in vogue during the early Christian era.

1. Egyptian Triad of Ramses II, Amon-Ra and Nut.
2. Egyptian Triad of Horus, Osiris and Isis.
3. Palmyra Triad of moon god, Lord of Heavens and sun god.
4. Babylonian Triad of Ishtar, Sin and Shamash.
5. Mahayana Buddhist Triune of transformation body, enjoyment body and truth body.
6. Hindu Triad *(Trimurti)* of Brahma, Vishnu and Shiva.

In the Hindu philosophy Lord Brahma is the Supreme God of Creation. Lord Vishnu is the Sustainer God. Lord Shiva is a God of Destruction. Hindus, who worship multiple deities, justify their dogma as monotheistic belief on the ground that each deity stresses one or more aspects of One Supreme God, called Brahma. There are hundreds of gods and goddesses in various Hindu temples throughout India. But each has its own specific power and place in worship, depending upon a particular aspect or aspects of the Supreme God that he or she stresses or represents.

THE EARLIER REJECTIONS

As seen before the early church was faced with serious problems that divided Christians in the third, fourth, and fifth centuries. The major reason for that division was the growing support for Arianism which defined God as *agenetos* -meaning derived from no source and the one that is ultimate source of everything. Arius advocated the 'Unity of God' and rejected the idea that Jesus was of same status as God the Father. The Logos ('word' meaning, Jesus) derived his being from God.

In 622 C.E., the Byzantine Emperor Heraclius adopted Monothelitism as a compromise between Monophysitism and the Orthodox Church. He advocated that Christ had one will but two natures. In 680 C.E., at Constantinople, this dyothelite stand of Jesus was condemned by the Church and the adherents were declared heretics. The doctrine soon died. A Church that had already adopted Trinity condemned Duality.

In the early sixteenth century, a group of the Baptist congregations rejected the idea of the Trinity in favour of the Oneness of God. The new teaching of these Unitarians spread in England, Poland and Hungary, and that alarmed both Catholics and Protestants. In 1553, Michael Servetus (Miguel Serveto) a Spanish doctor and theologian who advocated the Unitarian beliefs, was burned alive in Geneva for denying the Divinity of Christ (Incarnation) and the Doctrine of Trinity. The order was passed by John Calvin (Jean Cauvin), a great theologian who spread the Protestant Reformation in France and Switzerland. Calvin believed that biblical authority was above the Church tradition and yet he, who fought the Church for the sole authority of the Bible, passed an order for the burning of Servetus who was also fighting for the sole authority of the Lord. However, the Bible-based and reason-founded ethical 'Theism' of Servetus survived and in the latter part of the eighteenth century it spread into North America.

One group of Christians, founded in 1884 as an Unorthodox Christian sect, believes in One God who is Almighty and Supreme. They stress the imminent return of Christ but totally reject the doctrine of Trinity.

There are some denominations in the Christian community that believe in Trinity, but they say that the 'Three' (two Persons and one Spirit) are not co-equal. Father is the Supreme One, neither created nor begotten. Son is from the Father and begotten, but not equal. The Spirit is neither created nor begotten but proceeding.

Apostle Paul writes:

**For there is one God,
and one mediator also between God and men,
the man Christ Jesus.**
1 Timothy 2:5

THE RECENT REJECTIONS

Recently, two publications have caught my special attention, both are published from North America. The first to appear, *The Myth of God Incarnate*[28] is written by a group of Christian scholars. It says, "Jesus was (as he is presented in Acts 2:21) 'a man approved by God' for a special role within the divine purpose, ... and the later conception of him as God incarnate, the Second Person of the Holy Trinity living a human life, is a mythological or poetic way of expressing his significance for us".

---

[28] Philadephia: The Westminister Press. (1977).

Tom Harpur writes in his book *For Christ's Sake:*

> In fact, very few preachers can give a reasonable account of either the doctrine of the Trinity or the doctrine of the Incarnation, that is, that Jesus was truly human and yet fully God. They repeat formulae that were worked out, with much quarrelling and bitterness, in the fourth and fifth centuries by men whose need, outlook, and the understanding of the universe were vastly different from our own. These formulae are no longer useful-instead, they raise an insurmountable barrier for many who might otherwise become disciples of Jesus in our day.
>
> What is most embarrassing for the Church is the difficulty of proving any of these statements of dogma from the New Testament documents. You simply cannot find the doctrine of the Trinity set out anywhere in the Bible. St. Paul has the highest view of Jesus' role and person, but nowhere does he call him God. Nor does Jesus himself anywhere explicitly claim to be the Second Person of the Trinity, wholly equal to his heavenly Father. As a pious Jew, he would have been shocked and offended by such an idea.
>
> Over the last decade or so, I have talked as long and as frequently as possible about these particular doctrines with intelligent laypeople and clergy of all denominations, and I have found widespread confusion-in itself bad enough. But there is worse to come. This research has lead me to believe that the great majority of regular churchgoers are, for all practical purposes, tritheists. That is, they profess to believe in one God, but in reality they worship three. (page 7)

**Set not up with God another god,
or thou wilt sit condemned and forsaken.**
Koran 17:22

10
JOHN

**A disciple is not above his teacher,
nor a slave above his master.**
                              Matthew 10:24

THE "WORD BECAME FLESH"

In the New Testament the undermentioned verse is regarded as the cornerstone of the modern day Christology. I have repeated this critical passage (John 1:1), three times. Each repetition **(A-B-C)** is with a different insight and understanding.

    A. The text as it appears in the Bible.
    B. As it is understood by the Christian scholars.
    C. As it is understood by the Muslim scholars.

    **A. In the beginning was the Word,
       and the Word was with God,
       and the Word was God.**

B. In the beginning was Jesus,
and Jesus was with God,
and Jesus was God.

C. In the beginning was the Command,
and the Command was with God,
and the Command was God.

Thirteen verses after the above verse, the following text appears in the Gospel of John:

And the Word became flesh,
and dwelt among us,
and we beheld His glory,
glory as of the only begotten from the Father,
full of grace and truth.

In the Authorized King James Version, the words **"and we beheld his glory, the glory as of the only begotten from the Father"** are printed within the brackets, which clearly indicate that they did not appear in the original manuscripts but are added to the text to give credence to the theory of **"begotten from the Father."**

In the margin of the New American Standard Bible it is mentioned that **"the only begotten from the Father"** refers to **"Lit., an only or unique one or, an only begotten from a father."** This also indicates that the translator has taken the liberty of stretching the literal meaning of the original term **"unique one."**

The Koran teaches:

And they say, "God has taken to Him a son."
Glory be to Him!
Nay, to Him belongs all
that is in the heavens and the earth;....and when He
decrees a thing,
He but says to it "Be," and it is.

Koran 2:110

Here is an explanation of **"C"** above:

The **"Word"** that **"became flesh"** was a command from God, which said **"Be."** As a result of that particular command

- **Word** -, the conception of Jesus did take place in the womb of the Virgin Mary. In other words, the **"Word" ("BE")**, manifested into flesh. God himself did not become flesh. In the Koran, the "spirit" (Ar. *Ruh*) is called one of the Commands of God. Hence, it was the Holy Spirit (*Holy Command*) that did proceed from God and conceived. This philosophy is explicit and unreserved, and, does not conflict with any of the fundamental concepts of a monotheistic faith, and hence, you can **"Love the God, with all your mind."** Compare this concept with the verse from the Gospel of Matthew quoted below.

> **Joseph, son of David,**
> **do not be afraid to take Mary as your wife,**
> **for that which has been conceived in her**
> **is of the Holy Spirit.**
>
> Matthew 1:20

The Old Testament also supports the Koranic concept of God's Command **(spoken words)**, manifesting into things. In fact, that is how God Created His creation:

> **Then God said,**
> **"Let there be light";**
> **and there was light.**
>
> Genesis 1:3

FATHER AND SON

One who believes that God manifests or appears in three 'Persons' has to recognise conceptually that Jesus, the second Person of the Trinity, was, is and will be the eternal Son of his Father; everlasting to everlasting. That is to say, Jesus existed before his birth. This would be the reason why in John 1:1, a Christian would read *(by interpretation)* **"In the beginning was Jesus."**

Secondly, he must also recognize that Jesus Christ was complete in Godhead and complete in manhood, consisting of a reasonable soul and body; of one substance with the Father and begotten before the worlds as regards his Godhead, and of one substance with his Mother as regards his manhood. To be acknowledged in two natures, without confusion, without change, without division, and without separation. One person and one entity without being divided into two. Between the two there is no before or after, no greater or less.

The apostle Paul says:

> **But when the fullness of the time came,**
> **God sent forth His Son,**
> **born of a woman,**
> **born under the Law.**
>
> Galatians 4:4

The words **"sent forth"** clearly indicate there was an act of separation, or departure of one from the other. Secondly, the words **"God sent forth"** indicate that the Son was sent or commanded by the Father to go forth. This also establishes that there was a hierarchy between the Father and His son.

Jesus has confirmed the hierarchy in the following verse:

> **I glorified Thee on the earth,**
> **having accomplished the work**
> **which Thou hast given me to do.**
>
> John 17:4

The word Father means a person that is instrumental or helpful in the being of his Son. Even the biblical term **"begotten"** gives rise to the idea of Father having performed an act of procreation or begetting. It is immaterial at this point of discussion whether the act was physical or spiritual and when or how it occurred. If the act of begetting did take place, then the Son was not in existence before the action. If the act did not take place, then the term begotten is void. If term begotten does not mean what it says, then the phrase "Father and His Son" also does not really mean what it says. If the two are co-eternal and together from the very beginning, then why there is one called a Father, and the other a Son of his Father?

In John 20:17, Jesus said to Mary, **"I ascend to My Father and your Father, and My God and your God."** The words **My**

God tell us in *explicit and precise terms* that Jesus **"had"** a God, and was not himself a God. The text in John 1/1 reads; the Word was **"with God,"** hence the Word could not **"be God."**

> **Say: "He is God, One,
> God, the Everlasting Refuge,
> who has not begotten, and has not been begotten,
> and equal to Him is not any one."**
> Koran 112:1-4

11

PAUL

> Whoever then annuls
> one of the least of these commandments,
> and so teaches others,
> shall be called least in the kingdom of heaven...
> Matthew 5:19

EYEWITNESS TO THE GLORY

Paul, though not included among the 'twelve', was the largest contributor to the canonical text of the New Testament. Paul was a Hebrew and an Israelite from the tribe of Benjamin. He was also a Roman citizen from birth, using both the Hebrew name Saul and the Roman name Paul. He was not an eyewitness to the ministry of Jesus. Unlike the other apostles, he had not heard the sermons of Jesus, when Jesus insisted that the faith was to be based upon the Commandments that were inscribed in the Torah. Paul was an eyewitness to the glory of 'the risen Jesus', according to his own version. In the opening verse of his Epistle to Colossians, he declares himself **"an apostle of Jesus Christ by the will of God, and Timothy our brother."** Timothy was a son of a Jewess, Eunice. It is unknown when Timothy embraced Christianity. Paul chose him as his travelling companion.

Paul was a Pharisee; hence he was spiritually a Jew but intellectually a Greek, having been brought up in Tarsus. Politically he was a Roman citizen. When convicted by Jews as a heretic, he escaped being seized by hiding himself in a basket which was lowered from a window in a wall guarding the city of Damascus. (2 Cor.11/33). When his persuasions failed to convert Jews he stated, **"From now on, I shall go to the Gentiles."** (Acts 18:6). Jewish threats against his life forced him to flee and increased his hatred for Jewish traditions and laws.

THE LIBERTY FROM THE 'LAW'

Using the personality of Jesus, Paul liberated Christians from the observance of the Commandments by giving a new dimension to the 'Law'. The early Christians were Jews, observing the Jewish laws and traditions. When Paul and Barnabas argued with the people from Judea about their compliance with the Mosaic Laws, both were thrown out of the city of Antioch. Peter also clashed with Paul on the same subject.

Peter, who was also known as Simon, was one of the earliest students of Jesus. He was close to Jesus during his ministry, and Jesus had high expectations for him and his future mission. He gave him the name Peter and said:

> **And I also say to you that you are Peter (Gr., Petros, a piece of rock), and upon this rock I will build my Church...**
> Matt. 16:18

Peter was indeed like a rock, advocating the observance of the Commandments and covenants prescribed in the **'Law'**. His ideas on the subject are well recorded in the New Testament:

> **For it would be better for them (Christians),
> not to have known the way of righteousness,
> than having known it, to turn away
> from the holy commandment delivered to them.
> It has happened to them according to the true proverb,
> "A dog returns to its own vomit," and,
> "A sow, after washing, returns to wallowing in the mire".**
>
> 2 Peter 2:21-22

Those are very forceful words. Scholars believe that if Peter had prevailed over Paul the Christian traditions and beliefs would have been different from what they are today.

THE VEIL OF MOSES

Paul revolutionized the Jesus-advocated monotheism by giving a new dimension to Jeremiah's prophecy concerning the **New Covenant**. For details of the prophecy, please read Chapter 7, sub-heading "The New Covenant."

In his second Epistle to Corinthians, Chapter 3, Paul adds the innovative concept of **"Spirit of the living God"** to the prophecy. He believed the New Covenant prophesied by Jeremiah did not pertain to the Commandments 'written in ink' or written **"on tablets of stone"** but was of the Commandments written **"with the Spirit of the living God"** and written **"on the tablets of human hearts."**

Paul defines Christians as:

> **Servants of a New Covenant,
> not of the letter, but of the Spirit;
> for the letter kills, but the Spirit gives life.**
>
> 2 Corinthians 3:6

This is how Paul justifies his teachings:

> When Moses went to Mount Sinai he received two tablets of stone which were engraved with fire by the glory of the Lord. When Moses spoke with the Lord he was filled with the glory of the Lord and his face was brilliant. When he came

down from the mountain; **"the sons of Israel could not look intently at the face of Moses because of the glory of his face, fading *as* it was."** So Moses **"put a veil over his face that the sons of Israel might not look intently at the end of what was fading away."** (2 Corin. 3:7; 3:13)

Paul stretches his persuasion a little further:

> **But to this day whenever Moses is read,**
> **a veil lies over their heart;**
> **But whenever a man turns to the Lord [29],**
> **the veil is taken away.**
> **Now the Lord is the Spirit;**
> **and where the Spirit of the Lord is,**
> ***there* is liberty.**
> 2 Corinthians 3:14-17

What Paul is trying to rationalize is that whenever the Children of Israel and Judah read the Book of Moses, their minds were hardened because of the **'veil'** of Moses, which lay over their hearts. Then Paul says, **"the same veil remains unlifted, because it is removed in Christ."** (3:14). That veil **"is taken away"** by **"the Spirit of the Lord (Jesus)."** (3:16)

Paul not only provided the concept of the lifting of the **'Veil'** through the Spirit of the living God (Jesus), but also gave a notion that ***"there* is liberty"** through Jesus. He asked Christians to do away with the covenants of God, as demonstrated below.

THE COVENANT OF CIRCUMCISION

God made several covenants with Abraham. Some of these were everlasting covenants, or eternal Commandments. One of these was a covenant of circumcision.

> **This is My covenant, which you shall keep,**
> **between Me and you and your descendants after you:**

---

[29] Here the word 'Lord' refers to Jesus Christ (not Lord the God).

> every male among you shall be circumcised.
> And you shall be circumcised in the flesh of
> your foreskin;
> and it shall be the sign of the covenant between
> Me and you.
> And every male among you who is eight days old
> shall be circumcised throughout your generations...
>
> But an uncircumcised male who is not circumcised
> in the flesh of his foreskin,
> that person shall be cut off from his people;
> he has broken My covenant.
>
> Genesis 17:10-14

The Bible acknowledges that Abraham and his son Ishmael were circumcised together. History confirms that in the ancient times, any disregard for this divine requirement was punishable by death. In the Book of Exodus we find that Moses's wife Zipporah, **"took a flint and cut off her son's foreskin and threw it at Moses's feet"** (4:25), to avoid the wrath of God. Circumcision was an everlasting command, an eternal blessing for mankind.

The Koran explains that Islam is the religion of the patriarch Abraham. Every Muslim is expected to keep this Command of Allah made incumbent upon Abraham and his descendants. Muslims consider this Command of circumcision as a "Bestowed Favour" from their Creator. Allah knows what is good for His creation. Recently, it has been discovered that circumcision for males is hygienic and is best performed immediately after birth because of the higher percentage of the blood-clotting element present in the body at that time.

When Jesus Christ was confronted by Jews who wanted to kill him because he had **"made an entire man well on the Sabbath,"** Jesus counterquestioned the confronters by saying:

> ... and on *the* Sabbath you circumcise a man.
> If a man receives circumcision on *the* Sabbath
> that the Law of Moses may not be broken,

> are you angry with Me because
> I made an entire man well on *the* Sabbath?
>
> John 7:22-23

These words show that the Law of Circumcision was observed rigidly and word for word during his ministry. Jews were strictly following the command of circumcision on the "eighth day" after birth, even if it was on the Sabbath.

THE CONFLICT OF APOSTLES

After the death of Jesus circumcision became an issue for personal conflict between Peter, who insisted upon it, and Paul, who wanted the Gentiles to liberate themselves from the inherited Jewish traditions and covenants.

In Galatians 2:7, Paul writes:

> ...seeing that I had been entrusted with
> the gospel to the uncircumcised,
> just as Peter with *the gospel*
> to the circumcised.

The preaching of Paul prevailed. He revolutionized the Christian beliefs and traditions, creating new doctrines. The faith originally preached by Jesus was fundamentally different, and that has prompted some writers to name the Christianity revolutionized by Paul as "Pauline Christianity."

> **Circumcision is nothing,**
> **and uncircumcision is nothing,**
> **but (what matters is)**
> **the keeping of the commandments of God.**
>
> 1 Corinthians 7:19

Paul made a circumcision inconsequential and optional for Christians. But at the same time he said **"the keeping of the commandments of God"** was necessary and mandatory. This sounds like a self-contradictory statement. Circumcision was no doubt a **"Commandment of God"** the keeping of which should **matter.** And yet Paul says, **"circumcision is nothing"**!!!

Secondly, the covenants of the Bible are regarded as solemn agreements between God and his believers. Can an agreement be cancelled or cut short unilaterally without offending the other party? In the very words of God, is not an uncircumcised male **"cut off from his people"** because **"he has broken My covenant"**? (Gen.17:14).

Paul says:

> **And in Him (Jesus)**
> **you were also circumcised**
> **with a circumcision made without hands,**
> **in the removal of the body of the flesh**
> **by the circumcision of Christ**
> Colossians 2:11

> **Lord the God says:**
> **Every male among you who is eight days old**
> **be circumcised throughout your generations.**
> Genesis 17/12

Did the Omniscient Lord not know that Jesus would one day come into the world and pass away on the Cross; and in the process the **"removal of the body of the flesh"** become unnecessary for future generations? If He knew, did He err, when he used the words **"throughout your generations"** and **"in the flesh of your foreskin"**???

The Koran teaches:

> **Fulfil God's covenant,**
> **when you make covenant,**
> **and break not the oaths after they have been confirmed,**
> **and you have made God your surety;**
> **surely God knows the things you do.**
> Koran 16:93

'PAULINE JUSTIFICATION'

Paul advocated the idea that **"faith in Christ Jesus"** supersedes everything, including **'the Law'**. He writes:

> **...a man is not justified by the works of the Law**
> **but through faith in Christ Jesus,**

...by the works of the Law shall no flesh be justified.
Galatians 2:16

Paul believed that Jews and Gentiles could both gain acquittal by placing their faith in Christ Jesus. This rationale is known as **'Pauline Justification'**. Tom Wright writes, "Justification presupposes two things: sin and grace. No sin, no need for justification; no grace, no possibility of it." For a detailed explanation please read the next chapter.

THE PROPHECY FOR KEDAR

In the above 'Justifications' of Paul, I see one more reason that God said to Abraham, **"And of the son of the maid I will make a nation also."** (Genesis 21:13). It was a Master Plan of the Lord to make a new nation in the future, as soon as the older nations deviated too far from the original teachings and preaching of their prophets. The plain and simple commandments were transformed so much that the original message was lost in innovative double talk. The nation took it upon itself to decide what to obey and what to cast off.

Isaiah, whose wife is called the Prophetess, prophesied:

> **Behold, the former things have come to pass,**
> **Now I declare new things;**
> **Before they spring forth I proclaim *them* to you.**
> **Sing to the Lord a new song**
> ***Sing* His praise from the end of the earth!**
> **...Let the wilderness and its cities lift *their voices*.**
> **The settlement where Kedar inhabits...**
> Isaiah 42:9-11

Who was Kedar and which is the settlement of Kedar? There is only one person named Kedar (Hebrew *Qedar*) in the Bible. He was one of the twelve sons of Ishmael who settled in the wilderness of Paran (*Arabia*). (Genesis 25:13-15; I Chron. 1:29-31). Kedarites inhabited the Syro-Arabian desert east of Palestine in the northwest part of the Arabian Peninsula. In the Targums [30] and in rabbinical literature, Arabia

---

[30] An Aramaic translation of a Hebrew scripture reading. The translator had an option of making free interpretation. Some of these famous Targums are used alongside the original text.

itself is sometimes called "Kedar" - a land that Kedarites inhabit. The Koran is recited by Muslims like a poem in Arabic ("a new song").

Continuing the prophecy, the prophet Isaiah writes:

> **Let them give glory to the Lord,**
> **And declare His praise in the coastlands.**
> **The Lord will go forth like a warrior,**
> **He will arouse *His* zeal like a man of war.**
> **He will utter a shout,**
> **yes, He will raise a war cry.**
> **He will prevail against His enemies...**
> **And I will lead the blind by a way they do not know,**
> **In paths they do not know I will guide them.**
> **I will make darkness into light before them**
> **And rugged places into plains.**
> **These are the things I will do**
> **And I will not leave them undone.**
>
> Isaiah 42:12-16

Anyone who has read the history of pre-Islamic pagan Arabs and the advent of Islam would understand the finer points of the above prophecy. The words of **"His"** revelations, spread by the prophet Muhammad among the Kedarites (Arabs), did **"arouse 'His' zeal like a man of war"** among the converts. With a cry of *Allahu Akbar* (Allah is Great), they prevailed upon their powerful and influential enemies, the affluent merchants of Mecca. The teachings of the Koran led the idol-worshipping desert Arabs out of the darkness and guided them to light. Within a short period the **Glory** and the **Praise** of the Almighty Lord was declared "in the coastlands." All this was not the doing of a human being. It was what **"He"** had said **"I will do"** and **"I will not leave them undone."** It was done with the miracle of the Koran - 'the very words of God'.

Has the Koran prophesied what things He will do in the future? Yes. He will turn again unto men, meaning He will look upon mankind favourably and with "His" help **"...thou seest men entering God's religion (Islam) in throngs, then proclaim the praise of thy Lord..."** Koran 110:1

12
PERSONAL SAVIOUR

I, even I, am the Lord;
And there is no saviour besides Me..
                                    Isaiah 43:11

BELIEFS IN CHRIST

Thurman L. Coss [31] has very precisely and accurately described the three categories of Christians:

> I once knew a radiant and devout Christian lady who affirmed, with warmth and feeling, that for her Christ was a living presence in her life. She enjoyed, so she claimed, the knowledge that Christ was a spiritual power within her own heart. Her beliefs about Jesus were relatively few and straightforward. He was the Son of God, born of the Virgin, who lived and died on the cross so that sinful man could be saved. Being

---

[31] Coss, *Secrets from the Caves* (New York: Abingdon Press, Nashville) p109f

guiltless and sinless, Christ paid the debt for her sin, which she incurred as a descendant of Adam. Now that God's justice had been satisfied by Christ's sacrifice, the gates of heaven were opened to all who "knew Jesus Christ as their personal saviour." As far as she was concerned, she was certain that God had raised Jesus from the dead and that he ruled in heaven with God, as well as on earth in her heart and in the lives of like-minded Christians.

The reader will certainly be aware of a second and very large group of Christians who tend to think of Jesus in quite different terms from those described above. For them Jesus may have been a noble teacher, a prophet with moral sensitivity, and a man of courage who believed in God. They may see Jesus as a new Socrates willing to die rather than compromise a principle. He was a Jewish leader with a magnetic personality who attracted crowds because of his able use of the parable and because, in a few instances, his powerful personality actually overcame the fears of sick people in such a way that they were cured emotionally, and hence physically. Basically, his ideas and teachings came from Judaism, but with a few subtle refinements which distinguished the Galilean from earlier teachers and prophets.

These Christians would deny the Virgin Birth and the Resurrection. Indeed they would deny all supernatural dimensions in religion... They would not care to deny the genius and inspiration of Jesus, but they would suggest that other religious leaders have had similar gifts, and they would always want to compare Jesus' ideas with those of these others in an attempt to decide which religious leader is superior.

There is a third group of Christians who insist that the biblical faith is more than intellectual assent to a proposition, and even more than a new system of ideas and teachings. This third group puts emphasis on events in history. The Exodus and the Resurrection would be two such events. They suggest that biblical history is actually a story of God's saving and redeeming activity...God's purpose in all this activity was to lead sinful and presumptuous man back to obedience and a renewed fellowship between God and his people...

DEATH THROUGH 'ORIGINAL SIN'

The Christian idea of 'Salvation' is totally different from the concepts of the eastern religions. The entire process of mankind inheriting 'Original Sin' through 'a Son of God' and with it 'death', and then the loving Almighty God providing with His love 'a Second Son', who died for us, so that we all get salvation in his death, is not a concept easy to comprehend.

The Christian concept of 'Original Sin' or 'Adamic Sin' is based on the story of the 'fall' in the Garden of Eden. Adam was the first **"son of God."** (Luke 3:38). His wife Eve was deceived by Satan so that she ate a fruit from the forbidden tree. Eve gave the fruit to Adam, who also ate it. God sent both of them down upon the earth from the Garden of Eden. (Genesis Chapter 3). That was the Original Sin committed by the Original Son of God.

Paul views this 'Original Sin' from a different perspective. He writes in his epistles [32] that we all "fell down" and stand condemned to "death" because of the sin of Adam:

**Therefore,
just as through one man sin entered into the world;
and death through sin,
and so death spread to all men,**

---

[32] There is no Gospel ascribed to Paul. In the New Testaments there are letters *(Epistles)* written by apostle Paul. In the Koran, there is a recognition of the Gospel of Jesus (Ar. *Injil),* but none for the apostolic letters.

> **because all sinned–**
> **for until the Law sin was in the world**
> **but sin is not imputed when there is no law.**
>
> Roman 5:12-13

The doctrine of hereditary guilt and condemnation has formed a basis for much Christian theology. Let us hypothesize the plight of man if we were immortal:

(a) If Adam and Eve, and all that were born since, were immortal and yet producing immortal children, then countless billion children of Adam would be living on this planet. Some of those walking on our streets would be as old as 6000 years and others as young as 600 days.

(b) Accidents do happen. Countless millions would have broken their limbs, lost their vital organs, impaired their sight and hearing, damaged their brains and been made paralysed. There would be victims of the usual calamities such as fires, explosions, floods, earthquakes, combats, etc. All these unfortunate dismembered, deformed, disfigured and disjointed millions would be living in permanent misery and eternal anguish, with no hope for an end.

I think everyone would agree that immortality would have been the worst possible condemnation for the children of Adam. Ah! If there were immortality then Adam and Jesus would be alive to clarify the issues. But thinking of it, Jesus would not have died "on the Cross at Calvary" and the confusion would not have been created in the first place.

THE SECOND ADAM

John 3/16 is a verse that most Christians remember, as it is a base of the Christology.

> **For God so loved the world,**
> **that He gave His only begotten Son,***

> **that whoever believes in him should not perish,
> but have eternal life.**

Note: * In the margin of the text, it is mentioned that in the original Greek text, the word for **"begotten"** is **"Unique, only one of a kind."** (not begotten).

Paul, looking ahead from his new perspective, writes:

> **So then as through one transgression
> there resulted condemnation to all men,
> even so through one act of righteousness
> there resulted justification of life to all men.
> For as through the one man's disobedience
> the many were made sinners,
> even so through the obedience of the One
> the many will be made righteous.**
> Roman 5:18-19

Here is that one act of righteousness:

> **But God demonstrates His own love toward us,
> in that while we were yet sinners,
> Christ died for us.**
> Roman 5:8

Paul postulated that a baptized person is not only born again but also released from the **'Law'**, having died to that by which he was bound (the sin of Adam). The oldness of the letter of the 'Law' is over and the newness of the 'Spirit' has taken over. The theory is based on the old Hebrew theology in which the **"First Adam"** consisted of "flesh" and "life" *(bipartite)*. Paul added the third element of **Spirit** as a starting point from Jesus Christ, the **"Second Adam."**

ATONEMENT

That the Second Son of God (Jesus) was castigated in place of every born again Christian, yet to be born, is the base upon which stands the doctrine of Atonement. Jesus died on the Cross for the reconciliation of God and mankind. The doctrine of Atonement may lift up the image of Jesus but it certainly lowers the image of his Father. The very idea that

God Himself planned that His "Only Begotten Son" be mocked, tried like a common criminal, condemned, punished, forsaken, nailed to a Cross and murdered by his enemies to mitigate a sin or to satisfy His vainglory of Justice and the ego of Righteousness makes the Merciful and Compassionate Father not only a brutal parent but in human terms "Inhuman."

Fundamentally, the idea of 'Atonement' meaning "cover," "wipe off," "exchange" or at+onement (union - an act that enables mankind to be one with God again after having 'fallen') sounds like a speculative dogma or a hypothetical doctrine.

Even from a logical point of view, the system of belief advocated presupposes too many things and raises several questions, many of which have been asked by Christian scholars:

1. Why would a single act of disobedience by an individual, born thousands of years ago, make us all sinners?
2. How can a newly born child be a sinner? If he is a sinner then that sin is not of his doing or by his action. If God has so decreed, then that is not a sin but is an act of nature, for which the child cannot be held responsible like a condemned criminal.
3. Jesus was born 4000 years after the 'Original Sin'. What about the people who were born during those four millennia? Whose fault was it that Christ Jesus was not yet born? The heavenly Father is always conceptualized as a "Just" God. He would not do anything that is not equitable and evenhanded.
4. What about prophets like Noah, Abraham, Isaac, David and Moses? They too were children of Adam. Did they all die as condemned sinners?
5. If, for whatever reason or reasons, Jesus is truly 'Our Personal Saviour' or to be precise, the 'Only' Saviour, then why did God say, **"And there is no Saviour**

besides Me."? Did God intentionally misguide us or was He not aware of the future coming of Jesus?

MERCY AND JUSTICE

Within the attributes of God lies the admixture of Mercy and Justice. The sins of this world would greatly multiply if God was to look upon His creation with Mercy alone. Similarly the world could not endure if He decided on the basis of Justice alone.

The Koranic concept for Adam's act is totally different. The Koran reveals: **"And Adam disobeyed his Lord, and so he erred."** (20:119). Continuing further, the Koran says; **"Thereafter his Lord chose him, and turned again unto him, and He guided him."** This explains that Adam and Eve were absolved and favoured there and then. Allah would not carry that frustration or anger for 4000 years and then bestow His Grace through an act of cruelty - Crucifixion.

> **God created the heavens and earth in truth,**
> **and that every soul may be recompensed**
> **for what it has earned;**
> **they shall not be wronged.**
> Koran 45:21

Allah did not condemn mankind but said, **"We have honoured the Children of Adam...and preferred them greatly over many of those We created."** (Koran 17:72-73) He warned us like a loving Father: **"Children of Adam! Let not Satan tempt you as he brought your parents out of the Garden."** (7:26). **"...eat and drink, but be you not prodigal; He loves not the prodigal."** (7:29). And finally, He promised us that **"those who believe, and do deeds of righteousness"** shall be **"the inhabitants of Paradise."** (7:42).

> **Children of Adam!**
> **If there should come to you Messengers from among you,**
> **relating to you My signs,**
> **then whosoever is godfearing and makes amends–**

> **no fear shall be on them,
> neither shall they sorrow.**

AM I CONDEMNED?

> **He who has believed
> and has been baptized shall be saved;
> but he who has disbelieved shall be condemned.**
>
> Mark 16:16

In the Christian belief of 'Salvation', one is supposed to have faith in "Our Lord Jesus" as "Our Only Saviour."

Will I be condemned because I have placed my faith in the Almighty God (alone) as my Saviour and have not believed in Jesus as my Only Saviour or a Saviour besides God?

The answer to the question is twofold:

1. I have denied Jesus as my Saviour, but I have not **"disbelieved"** Jesus. The Koran insists that a Muslim must believe in the Virgin birth of Jesus Christ, in his miracles and in his prophethood, which I do. Please read the above verse and John 3:16 once again. Where does it say, "as my Only Saviour" or "as God incarnate"? Similarly, please go through the wordings of the text used in the ceremony of Baptism. Does it have the words "as my Only Saviour"? The baptism originally performed by John in the river Jordan was based on the Confession of Sin. (Matthew 3:6). Please read the verse printed in the beginning of this chapter (Isaiah 43:11). Does it not unequivocally negate the belief that Jesus is a Saviour?

2. I have not only believed in Jesus as one of the prophets from Almighty God but I have also believed in what he prophesied as an authoritative prophet. What good is a disciple *(student)* that says he has believed in his master as a trustworthy master, but does not believe in the "words" of his master? I am sorry to mention that Christians have known Jesus as their Saviour but have

not "known" what Jesus *told them as the truth, to their own advantage,* before his departure.

> **But I tell you the truth,
> it is to your advantage that I go away;
> for if I do not go away,
> the Helper shall not come to you;
> but if I go, I will send Him to you.
> And He, when He comes, will convict the world
> concerning sin, and righteousness, and judgment.**
>
> John 16/7-8

If you think **"Helper"** ("Paracletos" or "Comforter"), is the Holy Spirit then you are mistaken, because the Holy Spirit was already present at the time of the baptism of Jesus (Luke 3:22), and even before. Jesus was talking of someone (**"He"** not "it"), that was yet to come. Please read Chapter 16 of this book to know more on the subject.

MY ABANDONED SAVIOUR

Even in this century we sometimes read in the newspapers or watch on our television screens that a self-claimed "Divinity" is worshipped as a living god. It was not in the distant past that people believed that Emperor Hirohito of Japan and the Dalai Lama of Tibet were god(s). There are followers of Bahaullah who believe that their leader was 'the promised one' - an incarnation of Jesus. The devotees of Bhagwan Rajneesh believe that their Guru is an *Avatar* (Skr. Lit., descent) of God. In the past, people have given their lives in response to the words of such claimants. The most recent example is that of Reverend Jim Jones of Guyana. To an outsider all such claims seem hollow or fictitious. But, for an insider, his total submission to such claims is his most cherished and sacrosanct possession, a guaranteed key to Salvation. I can speak on this subject with complete confidence, on the basis of my own experience.

I believed, very strongly and gratifyingly, for most of my life, that one of the richest man in Europe, the Aga Khan was "a Living God." He had claimed "Supreme Divinity" for himself in his documented commandments of 1885, 1893 and 1903 and had asked his followers - Ismailis, [33] to make a firm commitment with their hearts to accept him so, and I so believed. I used to testify Aga Khan as: "Truly God" (*Ali sahi Allah*) in my daily prayers, three times a day. Aga Khan had personally assigned the text of ritual prayers for Ismailis. I sincerely believed Aga Khan was my Only "Saviour" (*Taranhar*), because in 1910 he had said in his published Commands (*Farmans*), "Heaven and Hell is in my hand."

In 1957 the old Aga Khan III died and his grandson Karim became Aga Khan IV. He accepted certain sums of money from me as part of our religious ceremony and said into my ear: **"I have forgiven your sins,"** after sprinkling "Holy" water on my face. All of us who have gone through that ceremony have been assured by our religious documents that on the Day of Judgment, Allah would not question us for our sins, committed prior to the ceremony. The important question is, were our sins truly forgiven because we had put our complete trust in our *Imam* (Spiritual Leader) as our *Taranhar (Saviour)?*

And who shall forgive sins but God?
Koran 3:130

As a Muslim it was my primary duty to verify from the Koran what the Aga Khans had claimed, assigned and said. Was I allowed to idolize, worship or venerate anyone as an intercessor or as a divine manifestation of God or God Incarnate? The Koran has forewarned that not only would I be committing an unpardonable sin, but that all such upon whom people call, besides Allah, will leave them in the lurch. (7:37).

In the December 1983 *Life* magazine, to the utter surprise of most of the Ismailis, Karim Aga Khan disclaimed being "a living god" and "the spokesman for almighty Allah." He did this in the strongest possible terms, through his Secretariat.

---
[33] Ismailis, the followers of the Aga Khan, constitute less than 0.2% of the total strength of the Muslim Brotherhood. To know more about Ismaili beliefs, history of Aga Khan's ancestary and his claim for spiritual leadership, please read *Understanding Ismailism* written and published by the author and publisher of this book.

In 1986, before a High Court In England, a statement was filed through solicitors in a legal dispute, which acknowledged that "neither the Aga Khan nor his grandfather had ever laid claim to divinity." I do not have to spell out what went through the minds of Ismailis after reading the above words, having also read the *Farmans* (commandments) of Aga Khan III and having gone through the ceremonies of 'sin forgiving' by the present Aga Khan.

I was a born Ismaili. Like most men of religion, we got "our" religion from our parents. Our beliefs are based upon that which we inherited or were taught in childhood. What if our parents were misguided to begin with? Or, what if they were not open-minded enough to look outside of their own circle? Do we all adopt the same professions or trades as our parents or approach our secular needs on their advice without assessing the pros and cons?

> ...and when it is said to them,
> "Follow what God has sent down,"
> they say, "No; but we will follow such things
> as we found our fathers doing."
> What? Even though Satan were calling them
> to the chastisment of the burning?
>
> Koran 31:21

I studied the history of Aga Khan's ancestry and when I was convinced that the Aga Khans were not the legitimate hereditary descendants of the prophet Muhammad and their teachings were not in accord with the Koran, I stopped running in the footsteps of my parents.

The paradox of this life is that well-informed and judicious non-believers in "Divine Supremacy," be it for Jesus or Aga Khan or any other individual, would express their compassion and pity for the misguided and deluded believers. Whereas, the so called "enlightened" believers, who take pride in attributing "Total Divinity" to a mortal being without understanding their own scriptures, would sincerely pity the non-believers and pray for their souls. Furthermore, their prayers for "enlightenment" would be addressed to the same

Jesus or Aga Khan.

Notes: 1. The words "Jesus or Aga Khan," as used in the above paragraph, do not insinuate or imply that the two are equal or similar. Jesus was a chosen prophet of the Lord. The Aga Khan is not a prophet or even a messenger or a spokesperson of God by his own admission.

2. Karim Aga Khan has disclaimed "Divinity" before the media but not before his followers. He has not as yet discontinued the ceremony of sprinkling "Holy" water. Similarly the followers continue the practice of reciting the hymns and prayers that attribute "Divinity" to Aga Khan. An Ismaili would tell you that Karim Aga Khan *is not God* as far as his physical body is concerned but Aga Khan *is God* as far as the spiritual manifestation of the *Noor* (Light) of Allah within his physical body. One Aga Khan but two aspects, one that is seen is called ***Zaheri*** and the other which is unseen is called ***Batini,*** explicates the Aga Khan in his various discourses and sermons.

13
"THE WAY" NOT "THE DESTINATION"

> God changes not what is in a people,
> until they change what is in themselves.
> Koran 13:11

Y. H. W. H.

The God of the Essene was an awe-inspiring figure. His personal name was considered too sacred to be pronounced with a human tongue and too holy to be written down. Four dots or four constants *Tetragrammaton*, written from right to left, (transliterated as Y.H.W.H. or Y.H.V.H.), represented the name of their God, usually rendered as Yahweh or Jehovah. Later, whenever the ancient Jews heard the Divine name from the mouth of their high priest, they used to kneel and bow down saying Blessings and Glory to the name.

From that extreme, Christianity went to the other. A mortal body of a young girl gave birth to God. Traditionally, the child was born on the first day of the first year of the Christian calendar, in Bethlehem. Many scholars believe he was born two to eight years before and probably not in Bethlehem. But these controversies are of no significance at this point. That child born of the Virgin Mary grew up to be known as Christ Jesus. He was *Meshiach*, a Hebrew term meaning "Anointed One." In Greek, the word for Messiah is *Khristos* or Christ.

His disciples and followers called him "a teacher" and "a prophet" like all other prophets that came before. His mission was neither self-glorification nor abolishing the 'Law' (Torah). He came to establish the 'Law' and to glorify the Heavenly Father. The essence of his message is in Matthew 5:17 to 20 and 7:21. Jesus began his ministry with his Sermon on the Mount (Matthew Chapter 5 to 7); which alone can be identified as the Gospel of Jesus, according to Jesus.

After his death, he was declared God Incarnate or God manifested as 'Person' by his own followers, or rather by the Church of his followers, although not once did he claim to be equal of his Creator. Of all the prophets of the Near East, his ministry was the shortest but his personality has been the most sentimental element in the religion that took his name.

A SECOND OPINION

I would like to present a second opinion on the subject from a totally different angle. Professor F. E. Peters, a professor of History and Near Eastern Languages and Literatures at New York University, writes in his book *Children of Abraham*.[34]

> The scrolls have been extensively scrutinized for insights into Christian origins, and interesting light has been shed on a number of questions - on John the Baptist, for example. But the overwhelming lesson of the scrolls for Christianity is that Jesus and his movement can be firmly located as a fairly ordinary type of Jewish

---

[34] Princeton University Press, Princeton, New Jersey (1982). p, 17

reform whose chief emphases were messianic and eschatological in character.

It is by no mean a simple matter to separate Jesus from his movement, a project of some importance, since it has long been felt by some that the early community of Jesus' followers shaped and may even have altered his teaching. The grounds for thinking this are two: the origin and form of the Gospels, and the change in the political and religious climate that occurred between Jesus' lifetime and the period when the Gospels were finally redacted.

Two pages subsequently, professor Peters writes:

On the Gospel testimony itself, his own followers were confused about the "kingdom of God," in what it consisted and when it would come to be. Jesus' audience was principally Jews, though occasionally he addressed both Samaritans and Gentiles, to the obvious and understandable distress of the Pharisees. The Jewish response to Jesus ranged from bewilderment to great and public enthusiasm. He obviously made a deep impression on many of his Jewish contemporaries, but the circumstances of his death apparently cooled the ardor of some.

"I AM THE WAY"

There are some verses in the New Testament that we often hear.

>...I (Jesus) am the way,
>and the truth, and the life;
>and no one comes to Father,
>but through me
>
>John 14:6

Jesus is **"the way,"** but Jesus is not "the destination." The **"words"** (teachings and commandments) of Jesus are **"the**

means" of an approach to his Father. But he is not the Father. Let me put this in the very words of Jesus: **"If anyone loves me, he will keep my word; and my Father will love him"** (John 14:23), and **"If you keep my commandments, you will abide in my love; just as I have kept my Father's Commandments, and abide in His love."** (John 15:10)

Two other verses often quoted are John 10/30 and 38: **"I and the Father are one."** and **"...Father is in me, and I in the Father."** Do these verses really mean that Jesus was or is, the "same" as the Father? Please turn a few pages further of the Gospel and read John 17/21 and 22. Here Jesus has used the same phrase for his disciples, after passing his glory to them. Are the disciples of Jesus, to be regarded as the "same" as Jesus and consequently, the "same" as the Father?

Paul writes in the first verse of his First Epistle to Timothy: **"God our Saviour"** and **"Christ Jesus, *who is* our hope."**

EXPLICIT MESSAGES

In contrast to the equivocal and cryptic quotations upon which the Christian faith is based today, here are few explicit **"words"** of Jesus. These messages are so clear and precise that they need no explanation:

> **Teacher, what good thing shall I do that I may obtain eternal life?**

Jesus replied;

> **...if you wish to enter into life, keep the commandments.**
> (Matthew 19:16-17)

When a certain ruler questioned Jesus, saying

Good Teacher, what shall I do to obtain eternal life?

Jesus replied:

> **Why do you call me good? No one is good except God alone.**
> Luke 18:18-19

When Jesus was tempted by Satan, Jesus answered:

> **It is written,**
> **"You shall worship the Lord your God and serve Him only."**
>
> Luke 4:8

The apostle John was one of the twelve that accompanied Jesus through almost all his ministry. In his writings he confirmed that he was an eyewitness to many events. He was a disciple loved by Jesus, as attested by Peter. John has testified in his Gospel how Jesus spoke of himself:

> **Truly, truly, I say to you, a slave is not greater than his Master; neither one who is sent greater than the one who sent him.**
>
> **For I did not speak on my own initiative, but the Father Himself who sent me has given me commandment, what to say and what to speak.**
>
> **I go to the Father; for Father is greater than I.**
>
> **I can do nothing on My own initiative. As I hear, I judge.**
>
> **And this is eternal life, that they may know Thee, the only true God...**
>
> John 13:16; 12:49; 14:28; 5:30; 17:3

The Koran informs us that on the Day of Judgment, Jesus will bear witness to the effect that during his Ministry, he never asked anyone to take him and his mother as gods.

> **And when God said,**
> **"O Jesus son of Mary didst thou say unto men,**
> **'Take me and my mother as gods, apart from God'?"**
> **He said, "To Thee be glory!**
> **It is not mine to say what I have no right to.**
> **If I indeed said it, Thou knowest it,**
> **knowing what is within my soul,**
> **and I know not what is within Thy soul;**
> **Thou knowest the things unseen.**

> I only said to them what Thou didst command me:
> 'Serve God, my Lord and your Lord."
>
> Koran 5:116

"GOD IS WITH US"

I have also heard a verse which a Christian would say demonstrates that Jesus is "God with us."

> Therefore the Lord himself will give you a sign:
> Behold, a virgin will be with child and bear a son,
> and she will call His name Immanuel.
>
> Isaiah 7:14

The literal translation of **"Immanuel"** is "God is with us." But the phrase **"a virgin"** does not appear in the original Hebrew text. The word used is *'almah* meaning "a young women of marriageable age." The Hebrew word for Virgin is *bethulah*. In the margin of the above verse, the translator has mentioned: "Or, maiden" meaning the word maiden has been substituted with **"a virgin."** What is the justification for this substitution?

When a Hebrew text is translated into Greek, it uses the word *parthenos*, which has a dual meaning; a young girl or a virgin. The translators have chosen the later although it does not correspond with the original Hebrew text.

Biblical scholars have suggested that the prophecy was concerning the second son or possibly a third son of Isaiah by a Jewish maiden. It does not relate to Jesus or his virgin birth.

GOD DOES NOT PRAY

In Mark 14:32 and Luke 3:21; 6:12; 22:44 there are narrations which clearly record that Jesus was praying while being baptized by John the Baptist. And, during his Ministry, Jesus was found **"praying very fervently"** and **"spent the whole night in prayer to God."**

A person reading the above verses with an open mind can understand that God does not pray. Anyone that is not free of "prayers" is a slave of God. If a god was to pray then He would be praying to a higher God,[35] a notion unacceptable to any monotheistic religion. A devout Christian might say Jesus was praying for our sins and not for himself. Fine, accepted, but the fact remains that he had to beseech and implore "someone else" to get our sins erased. He of his own could not forgive our sins. This proves that he was anything but God.

This was not the end of our discussion with a believing couple, who had recently visited our home in British Columbia. They explained to me, Jesus was a servant of his Master and yet God. I asked for further clarification and they maintained that in the Bible there are many Gods. Jesus was God and yet he served the Almighty God. So I asked: "Who is the Holy Father?" The reply I got was: "The Father is the Almighty God - **King of Kings, and Lord of Lords.** Jesus is 'Lord' but not **'Lord of Lords'**. Jesus is 'King' but not **'King of Kings'. Lord Jesus was received up into heaven, and sat down at the right hand of God."** And, they quoted me (Revelation 19:16 and Mark 16:19) to prove that they were right.

This reminds me of my school days in Bombay when His Majesty The King George VI was the Emperor and Sovereign Ruler of British India. In those days, we also had dozens of native *Rajahs* (Lit., 'Kings') of the various Indian States. Amongst these *Rajahs*, some were called *Maharajahs* (Lit. 'Great Kings'). But, all these *Maharajahs and Rajahs* would take orders from a Viceroy appointed by King George. At the Royal pageants and parties, these *Maharajahs and Rajahs* would sit on high chairs, on either side of Their Majesties. The Emperor of British India, "the King of Kings," would sit on the most prestigious Royal throne. And, his word or a written communique would constitute a "Royal Command" for *Maharajahs and Rajahs.* A written submission or a communique submitted by these *Rajahs* to His Majesty the King would be called "a prayer."

---

[35] Karim Aga Khan goes to Islamic Mosques on Fridays and prostrates to Allah, along with other Muslims. Whereas his followers prostrate before his photographs and pray to him every day, in Ismaili *Jamatkhanas* (prayer halls).

14
RESURRECTION AND ASCENSION

And if Christ has not been raised,
then our preaching is vain,
your faith also is vain.

And if Christ has not been raised,
your faith is worthless;
you are still in your sins.

1 Corinthians 15:14 & 17

THE SACRED 'LIGHT' OF EASTER

Many of you must have watched on television, during the days of Easter, one lonely bearded Greek patriarch emerging from the Church of the Holy Sepulchre, just outside the old city wall of Jerusalem, with two huge lighted torches, one in each of his raised hands. A hugh crowd of faithful believers who have been waiting impatiently outside, surges forward with their small candles to light them from the Holy Fire. All the candles inside the Holy Sepulchre and in other Churches are put out to symbolize the darkness of the tomb or the death of Jesus on the Cross. Devout followers of Jesus believe that the Holy Fire brought out of this Holy Sepulchre, built on the location of the Crucifixion of Jesus and his tomb, is ignited every year on Easter Sunday by a miracle of his Resurrection. Jesus, who is the Light of the world, has been raised. The Light from the Holy torches must be carried to the altars of their own churches at the utmost speed and hence there is a struggle to light hundreds of individual candles at the same time. The joyful news of Resurrection of Christ Jesus is thus carried from the place of his suffering and his Resurrection to all the churches.

THE CRUCIFIED BODY

The Resurrection of the crucified body of Jesus Christ is the foundation of Christianity. The following is an extract from *The Christians* [36]:

> Christianity is the only major religion to have as its central event suffering and degradation of its god. Crucifixion was a barbarous death, chiefly used for agitators, for pirates and for slaves. Part of the victim's punishment was to be whipped, and then to carry the heavy crossbeam to the place of his own death...Jesus's body was put in a rock tomb (after being lowered from the Cross) on the Friday; and by Sunday, all sides agreed, it had vanished. The Jewish authorities were sure the disciples had stolen it. The disciples were sure that Jesus had risen from the dead. And so, with the Resurrection, the suffering of Good Friday gives way to the joyful renewal of Easter Sunday.

---

[36] Bamber Gascoigne, *The Christians* (London: Jonathan Cape Ltd. 1977). p,17 and 20.

The apostle Matthew has also recorded the rumour that was **"widely spread among the Jews, and is to this day,"** of the crucified body being stolen by the disciples at night, while the guards were asleep. For details and further particulars, please read Matthew 28:11-15.

RESURRECTION

The Resurrection of Jesus and his Ascension are two separate things. Jesus was Resurrected (Lit. *came back to life again*) on the third day after his crucifixion. There is a difference of opinion between the apostles as to the exact date. But, all the four Gospels have recorded the physical Resurrection of Jesus in the same body, after being laid in the tomb.

1. Luke tells us that when the Resurrected Jesus appeared before his disciples and **"stood in their midst"** they were all **"startled and frightened,"** so Jesus tells them:

   > **See my hands and my feet,**
   > **that it is I myself;**
   > **touch me and see,**
   > **for a spirit does not have flesh and bones**
   > **as you see that I have.**
   >
   > Luke 24:39

   The disciples thought **"they were seeing a spirit (Ghost),"** so Jesus asked for something to eat. They gave him **"a piece of broiled fish**[37]**; and he took it and ate it in their sight."** (Luke 24:42-43).

2. When Thomas, one of the twelve disciples, doubted the rising of the Jesus (in a human body) and wanted to feel with **"His hands the imprint of the nails"** on the

---

[37] The words "and of an honeycomb", which do appear here in the older texts, have been expunged.

hands of Jesus and the mark made by a soldier's spear on his side, Jesus said to Thomas; **"Reach here your finger, and see my hands; and reach here your hand, and put it into my side; and be not unbelieving, but believing."** (John 20:27)

Note: Often we hear that Jesus had foretold his Resurrection to his disciples. If it was so, then why were the disciples **"startled and frightened"?** Why did disciple Thomas wanted to feel the imprints of nails before acknowledging the Resurrection of his master?

From the above one thing is certain: that Jesus did confirm by his own words and deeds that he had appeared in the same old physical body after his crucifixion. In other words the transformation was not from physical to spiritual existence.

Jesus was either safeguarded in the same body by an unknown factor or factors and escaped his death on the Cross at Calvary, or was revived (Resurrected) in the same body.

Many Christians also believe that Jesus had 'conquered' death by *raising himself* on the third day from the tomb. Jesus did not raise himself but **"The God of our fathers raised up Jesus, whom you had put to death by hanging him on a cross."** (Acts 5:30).

ASCENSION

Most of the apostles are not specific as to the date of the actual event of the Ascension (Lit. *act of moving upward*). John has recorded that Jesus was seen by his disciples eight days after his Resurrection, and that thereafter he performed a miracle of catching fish. The other three apostles have recorded the same miracle as being performed by Jesus with the same people and at the same lake early in his ministry. Paul says he was seen by over 500 people before he was raised up to his Father. The Acts of the Apostles has recorded that Jesus was seen forty days after his Resurrection.

...and for their saying,
"We slew the Messiah,
Jesus son of Mary, the Messenger of God" –
yet they did not slay him, neither crucified him,
only a likeness of that was shown to them.
Those who are at variance concerning him
surely are in doubt regarding him;
they have no knowledge of him,
except the following of surmise;
and they slew him not of a certainty–no indeed;
God raised him up to Him;
God is All-mighty, All-wise.

Koran 4:154

15
MIRACLES

> For you shall not worship any other god,
> for the Lord, whose name is Jealous,
> is a jealous God.
>
> Exodus 34:14

MIRACLES OF BIBLICAL PROPHETS

One noticeable difference between Christianity and Islam is that a Muslim does not build his faith upon miracles. Whereas, in the Christian faith the miracles of Jesus are glorified to such an extent that the faith of the majority of Christians is practically based upon them.

Even today, devout Christians look forward to the media-reported miracles that are said to be performed by statues of Mary in different parts of the world. Dozens of TV evangelists brag about demons being cast out and miracles performed in the name of Jesus to increase the membership of their evangelical clubs. Do you know what Jesus will say on **"that day"** to these "performers of miracles"?

> **Many will say to me on that day, "Lord, Lord,
> did we not prophesy in your name,
> and in your name cast out demons,
> and in your name perform many miracles?"
> And then I will declare to them,
> "I never knew you;
> DEPART FROM ME,
> YOU WHO PRACTICE LAWLESSNESS."**
>
> Matthew 7:22-23

According to the Bible, most of the biblical prophets performed miracles during their times, some even surpassing those of Jesus. But none of these prophets are worshipped or idolized like Jesus because of their miraculous powers. Listed below are a few:

Prophet Joshua commanded the sun and the moon to stop for one whole day. Moved a shadow of the sun-dial ten degrees backward (Joshua 10:13 and 2 Kings 20:10).

Prophet Elisha brought back to life a dead son of a Shunammite woman. Resurrected himself. After being dead and buried, he stood up on his feet. Healed a Syrian named Naaman of leprosy. (2 Kings 4:35; 13:21 and 5:14)

Prophet Ezekiel made the dry bones come together, grow flesh, cover with skin and come to life. (Ezekiel 37 3-10).

Prophet Elijah brought back to life a son of a widow. Made a bowl of flour and a jar of oil inexhaustible for many days. (1 Kings 17:22 and 14)

A King of Salem called Melchizedek was born without father, without mother, without genealogy and was made to live perpetual life like the Son of God. (Hebrew 7:3)

Solomon was there from the beginning, from the earliest times of the earth with God. (Proverbs 8:22)

Without going into the authenticity of these occurrences and the involvement of human factors in recording them, we will go to the next topic, the miracles of Muhammad.

MIRACLES OF MUHAMMAD

Huston Smith was a professor of Philosophy at Washington University. He writes in his book, *The Religions of Man* [38]:

> In an age charged with supernaturalism, when miracles were accepted as the stock-in-trade of the most ordinary saint, Muhammed refused to traffic with human weakness and credulity. To miracle-hungry idolaters seeking signs and portents he cut the issue clean: "God has not sent me to work wonders; He has sent me to preach to you. My Lord be praised! Am I more than a man sent as an apostle?" From the first to the last he resisted every impulse to glamorize his own person..."I am only a preacher of God's words, the bringer of God's message to mankind." If signs be sought, let them be not of Muhammed's greatness but of God's, and for these one need only open one's eyes. The heavenly bodies holding their swift silent course in the vault of heaven, the incredible order of the universe, the rain that falls to relieve the parched earth, palms bending with golden fruits, ships that glide across seas laden with goodness for man - can these be the handwork of gods of stone? What fools to cry for signs when creation harbours nothing else! In an age of credulity, Muhammed taught respect for the world's incontrovertible order which was to awaken Muslim science before Christian. Only one miracle is claimed, that of the Koran itself. That he by his own devices could have produced such truth - this was the one naturalistic hypothesis he could not accept.

---

[38] Published by Harper and Row (1985). p,198

OTHER MIRACLES

An exemplary Hindu from India would say his favourite *Murti* (statue of a Hindu god or goddess) works miracles for him and that that particular carved image in stone is his "god." A monotheist would resent the idea of worshipping an idol. Some misguided Muslims do offer prayers and pay their homage at various *Mazars* (mausoleums) of renowned sages to seek favours and protection. They would say their wishes are being fulfilled by the blessings *"barakah"* of the dead person. But, a devout Muslim would say that even to entertain an idea of seeking assistance from or praying to others besides Allah constitutes *Shirk* - a grave sin. A steadfast Ismaili, who prays and prostrates before the coloured photographs of his *Imam* (Spiritual Leader), would confirm that his daily supplications are being answered by his Aga Khan who lives in France.

Tom Harpur works as a nationally syndicated columnist on religion and ethics for a leading newspaper in Canada. He writes:

> Throughout history there have been shamans, medicine men, yogis, and healers of various kinds who have undoubtedly been able to effect astonishing cures. Having covered the phenomenon of faith-healing as a journalist, I am persuaded that such "miracles" do occur (sometimes in spite of the character of the healer concerned).[39]

An individual that goes after the transitory miracles is certainly overlooking the immutable, infinite miracles that are ceaselessly being performed all around and within him by his Creator.

---

[39] Harpur, *For Christ's Sake,* (Toronto: Oxford University Press, 1986). p,66

16
PROPHECY BY JESUS

**And when Jesus son of Mary said,
"Children of Israel,
I am indeed the Messenger of God to you,
confirming the Torah that is before me,
and giving good tidings of a Messenger
who shall come after me,
whose name shall be Ahmad."** [40]

Koran 61:6

THE "HELPER"

The prophets of the Old Testament, Moses, Jeremiah and Isaiah, foretold the arrival of a prophet like Moses. The question is why the Children of Israel and Judah who have studied and read these prophecies have recognized neither Jesus nor Muhammad as a messenger of God like Moses. Is it their social vanity or tunnel vision that is restricting them from looking outside?

---

[40] At the end of this chapter there is an explanation for the prophecy by name.

Upon examining the New Testament we find that Jesus Christ also foretold of the coming of another "Helper" like himself after his departure to the Father. The question is, why Christians who have studied and read that prophecy of Jesus, have not found another Helper like Jesus

Here are some of the statements of Christ Jesus, prophesying the coming of "another Helper":

**And I will ask the Father,
and He will give you another Helper***

**He shall glorify Me;
for He shall take of Mine,
and shall disclose *it* to you.**

**He will teach you all things,
and bring to your remembrance all
that I said to you.**

He will bear witness of me.

**He will guide you into all the truth;
for He will not speak on His own initiative,
but whatever He hears, He will speak;
and He will disclose to you what is to come.**

John 14:16; 16:14; 14:26; 15:26; 16:13

Note: *The original word used in the Greek text for "Helper" is Paracletos, which is also translated as Comforter, Mediator, Intercessor and Advocate.

Please note in all these quotations that the pronoun used is **"He,"** meaning a male person. A vital question remains: Did Jesus leave behind other identifying signs and clues for recognizing this other Helper?

A decade ago I wrote to the Vancouver School of Theology requesting further particulars of the word **"Comforter,"** from the original Greek text. On February 5, 1979, Dr. J. M. Lindenberger of this school of theology (affiliated with the University of British Columbia), wrote to me in his letter as under:

vancouver school of theology
6000 iona drive, vancouver, b.c. V6T 1L4 / (604) 228-9031

John 14:16-17

"Comforter"--The word in the original Greek text is παράκλητος (pronounced paráklētos). Its original meaning in Greek is "someone called to give aid to someone else", and the translators who rendered the New Testament into Latin used the word advocatus. Elsewhere in Greek literature, the word is used with the sense "mediator, intercessor, helper", etc., and that is evidently the sense in John 14. The word has no equivalent in Hebrew; in fact the Greek word is found as a loan-word in first-century (A.D.) Hebrew. For further discussion of the word and its usage, see W. F. Arndt and F. W. Gingrich, A Greek-English Lexicon of the New Testament and Other Early Christian Literature (Chicago: University of Chicago Press, 1957), p. 623b. For a discussion of the significance of the word in the context of John's Gospel, see Raymond E. Brown, The Gospel According to John XIII-XXI (Anchor Bible, vol. 29A; Garden City, N.Y.: Doubleday, 1970), pp. 643-44.

"Spirit of Truth"--Greek τό πνεῦμα τῆς ἀληθείας (to pneuma tēs alētheias). This corresponds exactly to a known Hebrew idiom, רוּחַ הָאֱמֶת (ruach ha-'emeth). The Hebrew expression does not appear in the Old Testament, but is found in the Dead Sea Scrolls, see G. Vermes, The Dead Sea Scrolls in English (Baltimore: Penguin, 1968), p. 75.

jml
5/2/79

affiliated with the university of british columbia

ANOTHER PARACLETE (ANOTHER JESUS)

On the suggestion of Dr. Lindenberger, I consulted the Anchor Bible, under the heading "The Gospel according to John (xiii-xxi)," volume 29A [41] and what I found was surprising.

The Anchor Bible is a project of international and interfaith domain; Protestant, Catholic, and Jewish scholars from many countries contribute individual volumes. Its object is

---

[41] Introduction, translation and notes by Raymond E. Brown, S.S., (Garden City, New York: Doubleday & Company, Inc. 1970).

to make the Bible accessible to the modern reader. Its method is to arrive at the meaning of biblical literature through exact translation and extended explanation. On page 1135 it is written:

> **The word parakletos is peculiar in the NT (New Testament) to the Johnannine literature. In I John ii 1 [42] Jesus is a parakletos (not a title), serving as a heavenly intercessor with the Father.**

The Anchor Bible continues:

> **Christian tradition has identified this figure (Paraclete) as the Holy Spirit, but scholars like Spitta, Delafosse, Windisch, Sasse, Bultmann, and Betz have doubted whether this identification is true to the original picture and have suggested that the Paraclete was once an independent salvific figure, later confused with the Holy Spirit.**

I would also like to add here that the word **'Spirit'** Gk., *pneu'ma;* is of a neutral gender and referred to by the pronoun **"it."** If the apostle John was referring to the "Holy Spirit" or "Spirit" as Paraclete then the pronoun used would have been **"it"** and not **"He."** Secondly, the Holy Spirit was already in existence and aiding Jesus when he spoke of the coming of another Comforter at a future date, *conditional to his departure* (John 16:7), and also *upon making a request to his Father.* (John 14:16).

On page 1141, the Anchor Bible states, after a detailed discussion, as under:

> **Thus, the one whom John calls "another Paraclete" is another Jesus.**

Note: The word **"another"** is very significant in the above prophecy. In the Greek text the word used is *"allon,"* which is the masculine accusative of *'allos'*.

---

[42] Quoted here is 1John 2:1 as a ready reference for the readers: **"My little children, I am writing these things to you that you may not sin. And if anyone sins, we have an Advocate (Gk. *Paracletos,* one called alongside to help) with the Father, Jesus the righteous."**

On page 1140, the Anchor Bible writes:

> **The identification of the Paraclete. If the Paraclete is "another Paraclete," this implies that Jesus was the first Paraclete (but in his earthly ministry, not in heaven as in I John ii 1). If the Paraclete is the Spirit of Truth, Jesus is the truth (xiv 6). If the Paraclete is the Holy Spirit, Jesus is the Holy One of God (vi 69).**

Listed below are some of the most significant identifications of the **other Paraclete (another Jesus)**, mentioned on page 1135 of the Anchor Bible.

1. **"He will glorify Jesus: (16:14)."**

    As seen in the previous chapters, Muhammad did glorify Jesus.

2. **"He will take what belongs to Jesus to declare to the disciples: (16:14)."**

    Muhammad become a prophet like Jesus. At the age of forty he declared his prophethood before the believers.

3. **"He will bear witness on Jesus' behalf, and the disciples too must bear witness: (15:26-27)."**

    Muhammad did bear witness on behalf of Jesus as to his birth through the Virgin Mary, his miracles and his prophethood. The Koran instructs every Muslim (disciples) to honour Jesus as a Messenger of God and believe in his virgin birth and his miracles.

4. **"He will speak only what he hears and nothing on his own: (16:13)."**

    The Book of Koran contains the revelations that Muhammad received through the archangel Gabriel. The Koran does not contain discourses held between Muhammad and his companions. [43]

---

[43] The sayings and discourses of prophet Muhammad are called *Hadith* (Lit. Speech). These reported sayings were collected and compiled in the first century and a half of Islam. There are six or more collections, out of which two are considered as *"as-Sahihan"* (the authentic ones). Any Hadith that is in disagreement with the Koran must be discarded.

5. **"He will guide the disciples along the way of all truth: (16:13)."**

Muhammad guided the Muslims to the way of monotheism, that is to believe in Allah (The God) alone, without associating anyone else as His partner or co-equal. And that in fact is "the way of all truth."

6. **"He will teach the disciples everything: (14:26)."**

Muhammad gave the Koran to the believers. The Koran is a complete guide by itself which teaches a believer about almost all subjects relevant to our lives, e.g. religion, politics, commerce, social science, marriage, sex, family life, laws of inheritances, history etc. Islam is therefore called 'A Way of Life'.

After quoting over twenty different passages connected with the word Paraclete and adding explanations of their own, the authors of the Anchor Bible write on page 1136:

> **Thus the basic functions of the Paraclete are twofold: he comes to the disciples and dwells within them, guiding and teaching them about Jesus; but he is hostile to the world and puts the world on trial.**

Fourteen hundred years ago when the prophet Muhammad came to this world, he was surrounded by pagan Arabs. These superstitious, wandering desert Arabs were not only idolaters but practised various customs that were immoral and sinful but yet were considered honourable. A new-born female child could be buried alive, and her birth brought shame upon the bearer. Birth of a male child brought honour and respect. It was an age of ignorance. Prophet Muhammad admonished these Arabs, reproved their practices and prevailed over his hostile enemies. The age of ignorance was over before his departure from this world. Then came the era of the Islamic civilization that led the way in the fields of mathematics, physics, chemistry, medicine, astronomy and geography.

Note: Before Ishmael was born, the Lord had spoken about the hostility. (Genesis 16:12). In Isaiah

42:10-16 the prophecy for Kedarites (Arabs) speaks of prevailing against **"His"** (Lord's) enemies.

If someone was to argue on the basis of John 14:26 that "the Helper" is "the Holy Spirit," I would like to mention that in the original manuscript discovered in 1812 on Mount Sinai by Agnes S. Lewis, the word mentioned is quite simply **"the Spirit"** and not Holy Spirit. For further detail please read *The Bible, The Qur'an and Science* by Maurice Bucaille.

In the Old Testament there is a prophecy by Jeremiah (28:9):

The prophet who prophesies of peace,
when the word of the prophet shall come to pass,
then that prophet will be known
***as* one whom the Lord has truly sent.**

The roots of the words Islam *("salam")* and Muslim *("aslama")*, mean "peace." When one Muslim encounters another, they greet each other by saying, *"as-salamu 'alaykum"* meaning, "peace be upon you." The Koran has foretold that the greetings in Paradise and the salutations by the angels will be *"as-salaam 'alaykum."*

Muslim scholars hold that the word Paraclete (pronounced parakletos) is a corruption of a Greek word *Periklytos*. In Greek or Aramaic (the language of the prophet Jesus) the word Periklytos means "the praised one." The name Muhammad means "he who is glorified or praised" and the name Ahmad (by which the prophet was also known) means "the most laudable."

The Koran has declared that the prophet Muhammad is the 'Seal' of prophethood, meaning there will be no more prophets after Muhammad. The Koran is to be regarded as the final and everabiding scripture for mankind. In other words, the guidance that Muhammad has conveyed is **to abide with mankind for ever.**

17
REPEATED SUDDEN CREATIONS

> Say: "Is there any of your associates
> who originates creation, then brings it back again?"
> Say: "God - He originates creation,
> then brings it back again;
> so how are you perverted?"
>
> Koran 10:35

CREATION OR EVOLUTION?

One of the most controversial subject from the Bible is to be found in the Book of Genesis. The opening sentence of Genesis reads, **"In the beginning the God created the heaven and the earth."** The moment you think of 'Creation', the word 'Evolution' trails behind like its shadow. Christians have not been able to resolve the age-old debate of Creation versus evolution. Biblical scholars have been faced with this question in their churches, in the schools and even in courthouses. Evolution as well as Creation has its own unsolved mysteries. Parties on both sides of this great debate are well aware of their dilemma. The Koran with its theory of repeated creations reconciles the two, especially in view of the most recent scientific discoveries. But, before we go into some serious discussion here are some interesting facts that I have picked up from *Blueprints Solving The Mystery Of Evolution.* [44]

> Just before 1650 a learned Irish archbishop, James Ussher, decided to calculate the age of the earth from evidence in the Bible. Working his was back through all the "begats," he concluded that Adam and Eve had been created by God in 4,004 B.C. Other scholars confirmed this finding. They even improved on it, pinpointing the actual moment of human creation at 9:00 A.M. on Sunday, October 23. This date thereafter assumed a heavy weight of authority. It became a baseline for measuring earthly time, a point at which scholarship and science met and blended with Church doctrine. Later geological evidence would have a hard time dislodging it. (This chronology prepared by archbishop James Ussher appears in some twentieth-century Bibles). (page 8).

> The clergyman was Samuel Wilberforce, Bishop of Oxford. He was a great public favourite, the producer of a stream of such smooth and oily sermons that he was nicknamed "Soapy Sam."...The event at which he was slated to demolish Darwin was the annual meeting of the British Association for the Advancement of Science, set for a Saturday in June 1860. This would be no routine, droning scientific exchange. It would be the first direct confrontation between the forces of the new evolutionary view and those of the entrenched view held by

---

[44] Edey & Johanson, (Boston/Toronto/London: Little, Brown and Company, 1989).

the Church and by catastrophist, fixed-species men like Owen. (Professor Huxley was to defend the Darwinian theory). (page 86).

"I beg to ask you, Professor Huxley, (questioned the Bishop) is it on your grandfather's or your grandmother's side that you are descended from a monkey?" There was an explosion of applause, under which Huxley turned to the man next to him and whispered: "The Lord hath delivered him into mine hands." (page 88).

"I assert that a man has no reason to be ashamed of having an ape for a grandfather. If there were an ancestor whom I should feel shame in recalling, it would rather be a *man* endowed with great ability and a splendid position who used those gifts to obscure the truth." (answered the professor). (page 89).

A GREAT DESIGNER

The human brain that was once so eager to accept the theory of evolution by natural selection or preservation of favoured races in the struggle for life, as developed by Charles Darwin and Alfred Wallace, finds it not so easy to do so now. Today, the brain knows that there are certain "scientific data" which it cannot ignore in order to refute the existence of a Great Designer. The brain is aware that a neurosurgeon can open the skull and show us on a television screen that there are over 10 billion nerve cells or neurons in that brain, each with hundreds of contact points or synapses capable of producing thousands of electro-chemical actions and reactions that convey individual messages through an intricate nervous system to the various body parts and organs to trigger precisely controlled harmonious functions.

Furthermore, it is an undisputed scientific fact that all these components and controllers were evolved out of a mixture of a drop of male fluid and a female fluid. This admixture carries a coded imprint. If the said coded imprints were to be written out in ordinary language, it would fill a hundred thick volumes. All these codes are set to perform billions of intricate interrelated acts at precise moments, harmoniously and from one end of the fetus to the other, so as to reproduce a nearly identical normal healthy human baby within approximately forty weeks of the conception. Today many people accept the idea of a "Great Designer" and the idea of evolution, saying that evolution was the process through which He created everything.

Fourteen hundred years ago, the Koran had told us:

We created man of a sperm-drop, a mingling*, trying him; and We made him hearing, seeing...
Koran 76:2

Note: *   The original word in Arabic for **"a mingling"** is *amsaj* which literally means "mingled liquids." The fertilization of an ovum takes place when a drop of the fertilizing agent, the male sperm (spermatozoon) mingles with it.

**"We created man of an extraction of clay,
then we set him, a drop, in a receptacle secure,
then We created of the drop a clot,
then We created of the clot a tissue,
then We created of the tissue bones,
then We garmented the bones in flesh;
thereafter We produced him as another creature,
So blessed be God, the fairest of creators!"**
Koran 23:11-14[45]

SUDDEN EXTINCTION

A question that has baffled scientists is why did dinosaurs became extinct? It has been established from the fossil records from different parts of the world (e.g. Alberta) that the disappearance of dinosaurs was seemingly very sudden and absolute. There are several theories put forward as to

---

[45] Suggested reading for detailed information on the subject of human reproduction and the scientific details in the Koran; Maurice Bucaille, *The Bible the Qur'an and Science* (Indianapolis: American Trust Publications, 1978).

why dinosaurs became extinct, such as, a comet or asteroid collided with the earth at a tremendous speed, the earth's magnetic field reversed, there was a supernova explosion, or there were extreme climatic changes, heavy acid rains or extreme food shortages due to any of the above events. Upon reviewing all these hypotheses it appears that nature has played an important part in the sudden extinction of dinosaurs from this planet.

SUDDEN ORIGIN OF NEW SPECIES

Stephen Jay Gould teaches, as he has for nearly two decades, geology, biology, and history of science at Harvard University. He writes in his book, *Hen's Teeth and Horse's Toes - further reflections in natural history:* [46]

> I count myself among evolutionists who argue for a jerky, or episodic, rather than a smoothly gradual, pace of change. In 1972 my colleague Niles Eldredge and I developed the theory of punctuated equilibrium. We argued that two outstanding facts of the fossil record - geologically "sudden" origin of new species and failure to change thereafter (stasis) - reflect the predictions of evolutionary theory, not the imperfections of the fossil record. In most theories, small isolated populations are the source of new species, and the process of speciation takes thousands or tens of thousands of years. This amount of time, so long when measured against our lives, is a geological microsecond.

In *Newsweek* March 29, 1982 appeared an article on the theory of punctuated equilibrium and the New Evolutionary Timetable by Steven M. Stanley, a Johns Hopkins' paleontologist. In brief it said.

Instead of changing gradually as one generation shades into

---

[46] New York/London: W.W. Norton & Company, 1980. p,259

the next, evolution proceeds in discrete leaps...There are no transitional forms between species, but rather a sudden emergence of new species...There are hypothetical 'missing links' from one species to another...This applies to Homo sapiens as it does to other species.

In 1985, professor Gould published *The Flamingo's Smile*[47]. He writes:

> If punctuated equilibrium dominates the pattern of normal times, then we have come a long way toward understanding the curiously fluctuating directions of life's history. Until recently, I suspected that punctuated equilibrium might resolve the dilemma of progress all by itself.
> I now realise that the fluctuating pattern must be constructed by a complex and fascinating interaction of two distinct tiers of explanation - punctuated equilibrium for normal times, and the different effects produced by separate processes of mass extinction. Whatever accumulates by punctuated equilibrium (or by other process) in normal times can be broken up, dismantled, reset, and dispersed by mass extinction. If punctuated equilibrium upset traditional expectations (and it did ever!), mass extinction is far worse.

The Koranic verses quoted below explain that Allah has been putting away the old creation (extinction!) and has been bringing in a new creation ("sudden origin"!) upon this earth in a fashion we know not.

**If He will, He can put you away
and bring a new creation;
that is surely no great matter for God.**

**We have decreed among you Death;
We shall not be outstripped;
that We may exchange the like of you,**

---

[47] Published by W.W. Norton & Company, New York and London. p 242.

> **and make you to grow again in a fashion
> you know not.**
>
> Koran 14:22; 56:60
>
> **On the day when We shall roll up heaven
> as a scroll is rolled for writings;
> as We originated the first creation,
> so We shall bring it back again –
> a promise binding on Us;
> so We shall do.**
>
> Koran 21:104

The above is not a conclusive theory or an accepted Islamic belief which has been published before. Allegorical verses can only be explored but cannot be claimed as facts. I have tried to visualize the picture, through some of the ambiguous messages of the Koran. But, the Koran teaches us:

> **It is He who sent down upon thee the Book,
> wherein are verses clear that are Essence of the Book,
> and others ambiguous...
> and none knows its interpretation,
> save only God.**
>
> Koran 3:5

18
COLLECTION OF SCRIPTURES

> When some affliction visits a man,
> he calls upon his Lord,
> turning to him;
> then when He confers on him a blessing from Him
> he forgets that he was calling to before
> and sets up compeers to God,
> to lead astray from His way.
>
> Koran 39:10

The history of the collecting of the Old Testament, the New Testament and the Koran in their original form (canons) is a fascinating one.

THE OLD TESTAMENT

Some two hundred years ago, while studying the undermentioned passage from the Book of Moses, Bible scholars noticed that what God said to Moses on Mount Sinai contradicted earlier texts. God obviously could not have lied to Moses nor could Moses have contradicted his own previously written text. This was a clue that Moses was not the author of both texts and the compiler(s) must have used more than one source.

In the Second Book of the Bible, Exodus 6:2-3, it is written that the Lord declared his personal name to the prophet Moses *for the first time.*

> **God spoke further to Moses and said to him,**
> **"I am the Lord;**
> **and I appeared to Abraham, Isaac, and Jacob, as God Almighty,**
> **but *by* My name, Lord,**
> **I did not make Myself known to them."**

The Bible scholars knew, upon reading the First Book of the Bible 4:26; 12:8 and 26:25, that the Israelites knew the expressed name of their Lord long before Moses. In fact, the name of Moses' mother was Jochebed, which meant "Yahweh is glory."

Any observant Bible reader would notice that there are two versions of the same story or event, narrated one after the other in the Old Testament. By the end of 19th century there was the general recognition of at least four main sources underlying the present Pentateuch (the first five books of the Old Testament).

1. **J** = Yahwistic Text. Source using Yahweh (representing 'Jehovah') as God. It was written in Judah in the time of David or Solomon.

2. **E** = Elohistic Text. Source using Elohim as God. It was written in Israel after the disruption of the old Solomonic kingdom.

3. **D** = Deuteronomy. The work of the Deuteronomist, written in the last quarter of the seventh and the

first quarter of the sixth centuries B.C.E..

4. **P** = Priestly Account. Source that took shape after Babylonian exile (586-538 B.C.E.). The first four books of the Bible were written by the priestly writers, who used both "J" and "E" texts and re-wrote some materials.

The scholars have also noticed that the 'J' or 'Y' text portrays God as anthropomorphic, i.e. human deity, whereas the 'E' text portrays a spiritualized God. The 'P' text is noted for refined theological expression. This could have been due to the personal preference of the narrator influenced by the traditional beliefs of the era. The essence is in the 'Message' itself and not how it is draped.

The next obvious question would be, How serious are the textual differences or disagreements between these repeated twin narrations?

Below are two texts, each describing the sequences of the Creation.

The first description:

"And God created the great sea monsters, and every living creature that moves,...and every winged bird after its kind; and God saw that it was good. And God blessed them, saying, `Be fruitful and multiply..." (This was the fifth day of the creation). **"Then God said, 'Let Us make man in Our image, according to our likeness; and let them rule over the fish of the sea and over the birds of the sky and over the cattle... and over every creeping thing that moves on the earth."** (This was the sixth day of the creation). (Genesis 1:21-31) God rested on the seventh day.

The second description:

"This is the account of the heavens and the earth when they were created,...Then the Lord God formed man of dust from the ground, and

> **breathed into his nostrils the breath of life; and man became a living being...Then the Lord God said, "It is not good for the man to be alone; I will make him a helper suitable for him." And out of the ground the Lord God formed every beast of the field and every bird of the sky, and brought *them* to the man to see what he would call them...** (Genesis 2:4-23)

The above two texts are inharmonious and conflicting in their account of the sequence of the creation of man. The first version states that man was created on the sixth day of the creation, when the birds, beasts and fishes were already created. The second version tells us that man was created before the creation of birds and beasts.

THE NEW TESTAMENT

The first three books of the New Testaments are the Gospels by apostles Matthew, Mark and Luke. They are known as Synoptic Gospels because they often agree with each other in subject, order and language. The fourth and last Gospel is by the apostle John. His Gospel contains no parables in the synoptic sense. The first three Gospels were written between 65 to 85 C.E. and the last during the period 60 to 100 C.E.

John's Gospel enjoys a very special place in the New Testament. It contains information regarding the early Judean Ministry of Jesus as well as extensive discourses by Jesus with his disciples that the other three Gospel have not recorded.

There is no evidence in the New Testament that demonstrates that Jesus recorded anything in his own hand. However, there is a term, the "Gospel of Jesus," in the New Testament which could simply mean the "Good news of Jesus," or could mean a book of Gospel, written or dictated by Jesus, which has been lost or destroyed. The apostle Mark has recorded:"**...Jesus came into Galilee, preaching the gospel of God."** (1:14).

The first book of the New Testament is the Gospel according to Matthew, and it begins with the genealogy of Jesus Christ. As in the Old Testament, there are two versions and they are in disagreement.

The apostle Matthew has recorded the following generations of Abraham by their names:

14 Generations from Abraham to David.
14 Generations from David to the deportation
    to Babylon.
14 Generations from deportation to Jesus.

The apostle Luke records as under:

15 Generations from Abraham to David.
20 Generations from David to deportation.
22 Generations from deportation to Jesus.

Bible scholars have explanations for some but not all of these variations. The ministry of Jesus lasted for a short span of time and yet there are textual variations between these four Gospels with regards to the timings of the incidents, the miracle of draught of fishes and overturning of the tables of the money-changers are the examples.

THE KORAN

At the beginning of the seventh century C.E. - nearly six centuries after the prophecy of "another Paraclete" by Jesus - the archangel Gabriel brought from his Master, the Almighty Lord, the first five verses of the Koranic Revelations and revealed them to the prophet of Islam - Muhammad, in a mountain cave outside Mecca, where he was meditating. This and later revelations, collected together, formed the Koran - the Islamic Holy Book.

The word Koran comes from an Arabic word *al-Qur'an* meaning "the Recitation," a reference to the recitation of the Divine Revelations. Muslims believe that the Messages of the Koran are God's own Words revealed for all mankind, not for Muslims alone. The Messages are eternal and universal. The

Koran is also regarded as the final scripture because no other scripture has since been revealed or shall be revealed.

After the first revelation in 610 C.E., the 'Revelations' continued to arrive in bits and pieces for the next 22 years. Whenever a portion of the Koran was revealed, the prophet would ask his close associates to write it down and recite. One of the better known scribes who took such dictations from the prophet was Zayd ibn Thabit.

After the passing away of the prophet in 632 C.E., his successor - *a Caliph* (the community leader, not another prophet) - asked Zayd to collect these recorded verses from the various individuals who had written them on the pieces of leather, wooden tablets, soft stones, leaves of palm trees and parchments. Later on, the third Caliph 'Uthman (644-656 C.E.) appointed a commission, headed by Zayd, to prepare a faithful copy from these collected verses. The definitive canon was established by the commission and a copy was prepared within the 23 years of the passing away of the prophet. The Caliph then ordered several copies to be made from the original and distributed to various distant Islamic centres. He then ordered that all the fragmented records of the revelations be burnt to avoid any confusion in the future. The copy of the Koran in Arabic that we see today is identical to the original collected by the commission 1300 years ago. Copies attributed to Uthman do exist in Istanbul and Tashkent (U.S.S.R.). The Koran was first translated into Latin circa 1143 and into English in 1657.

During the early years of Islam, the Koran was written in the old Arabic script, which did not have the diacritical marks on the constants denoting the vowels they would take. The Muslims of Arabia, whose mother tongue was Arabic, had no difficulty in reciting the verses written in the old script because they had heard them during ritual prayers and directly from the prophet. When Islam was spread outside of Arabia, the non-Arab Muslims (e.g. Persians) had difficulty reciting the verses without these diacritical marks. Often words were mispronounced and, unintentionally, that would lead to a different meaning or gender or tense of a verb. Hence these diacritical signs and marks for appropriate punctuation were introduced later. In some rare instances , placing a different sign on letter or using a comma instead of a period does alter the meaning of a verse, resulting in more than one interpretation (e.g. Koran 3:7).

The Koran is divided into 30 parts , 114 Chapters and has over 6200 Verses. The Koran has not been compiled in the same chronological sequence as it was revealed to the prophet. Generally speaking, the longer chapters are placed at the beginning and the shorter ones at the end. In the market one can find copies of the text printed in a chronological order. But, the chronological sequence is that of the Chapters and not of the Verses.

19
CONCLUSION

> Call thou to the way of thy Lord
> with wisdom and good admonition,
> and dispute with them
> in the better way.
>
> Koran 16:126

NATIONAL TRADITIONS & CUSTOMS

Recently a friend of mine sent me a newsletter.[48] The opening article read:

> One of the main reasons for the continuing of Idolatrous practices is custom. Just as nations have their own political, social and national customs, so they have their misguided religious customs. New ideas and practices are formed in the name of religion even though they may be completely opposed to the teachings of that religion...

---

[48] Newsletter No.55 (August 1989) published by, Islamic Cultural Centre, 146 Park Road, London.

> If these people are questioned concerning the validity of their practices, they reply that their families, tribes and ancestors have done so for centuries and so they are following in the footsteps of their forefathers...
>
> To follow your ancestors is not compulsory, and neither is it practical at times. Our ancestors included tyrants, blood-thirsty criminals and unjust leaders. Should we, their children, take it as part of our tradition to imitate their actions?
>
> Our ancestors rode on camels and horses, wore the skins of animals, worked on the land and did everything in a most laborious manner. By inventing and using cars, roads, machines and computers, we have rejected their traditions. No-one has ever disputed all the scientific advances being made around us, but when someone questions the 'religious' practices of forefathers and ancestors, it becomes a very serious issue indeed. The person is punished, not for disputing the religion, but for disputing the tradition, even though that particular tradition has no validity in the religion of the people.

The article identifies the customs that have been the root cause of deviation from the teachings of the Judaism, Christianity and Islam.

Jesus, while speaking of the religious trend-setters among his progenitors, was probably unaware of the trend-setting deeds of his own followers. Similarly, if the prophet Muhammad was to see some of the customs prevalent among the Muslims of today, specially in India and Pakistan, he too would be shocked. Jesus spoke of the dictators of such norms:

> **The scribes and the Pharisees [49] have seated themselves in the chair of Moses...And they tie**

---

[49] A Jewish sect that believed God was universal. They were anti-nationalistic, self-righteous and upheld strict obedience to a traditional interpretation of the Torah. Paul was originally a Pharisee.

> up heavy loads, and lay them on men's shoulders; but they themselves are unwilling to move them with *so much as* a finger...And they love the place of honour at banquets, and the chief seats in the synagogues, and respectful greetings in the market place, and being called by men, Rabbi...But woe to you, scribes and Pharisees, hypocrites, because you shut off the kingdom of heaven from men; for you do not enter in yourselves, nor do you allow those who are entering to go in...Whoever swears by the temple, that is nothing; but whoever swears by the gold of the temple, he is obligated. Whoever swears by the altar, *that* is nothing, but whoever swears by the offerings upon it, he is obligated. You blind guides, who strain out a gnat and swallow a camel.
>
> Matthew Chapter 23

The history of Judaism tells us that about seventeen centuries after the death of Moses the professional scribes *(soferim)* and rabbis constituted the heart of rabbinic Judaism. They introduced the Mishna - the corpus of legal and other matters. These rabbinical teachings became the basis for the Talmud. The Jerusalem Talmud was based upon Galilean Gemara (commentaries, traditions, history and folklore) and the Babylonian Talmud was based upon Iraqi Gemara. The combination of these two Aramaic commentaries along with the authoritative teachings of rabbi Judah ha-Nasi became a document of growing authority over the Torah (the 'Law'). The respect these rabbinic works gained, during the second and third century C.E. has guided Judaism since then. The religious courts of Jews have since then recognized them as unrivalled documents. The Koran tells us that Jews have imposed upon themselves several customs and practices that God never intended. They are self-imposed hardships.

From an Islamic point of view, if at any date in the future any categorized document of the reported *Hadith* (the sayings of Muhammad recorded centuries later on the authority of his contemporaries) [50] was to become a document of growing authority over the Koran, like the Talmud, then Islam would also be deviating from the path of true Islam. At times Muslims do impose upon themselves additional hardships and burdens that the Koran had never dictated. One does notice, on rare occasions, incidents of such improprieties and imposed hardships, but one has to think twice before raising one's voice against deeply rooted national customs and traditional practices and being labelled as a heretic. The trend of today's preaching, especially in the Western nations, is such that the teachings of the Koran will prevail in the course of time. The tendency is also to become "non-imitators" or "not attached to innovations" *(ghayr muqallidun)* Muslims. During the 8th and 9th centuries C.E. several schools of traditions promoting *usul al-fiqh* (foundations of sacred law) were developed and named after the individual scholars, such as Hanafi, Hanbali, Maliki, Shafii, Jafri, Zaydi.[51] Muslim society in the West is trying to unite them all. The base of their arguments lies in verse 6:71 of the Koran which says:

Say: "God's guidance (Koran) is the true guidance."

Christianity has been greatly influenced by the texts of the Epistles. They have often prevailed over the Gospel taught by Jesus. When John the Baptist **"had been taken into custody"** Jesus began his ministry from Galilee **"preaching the Gospel of God,"** meaning the "Good News of God's Kingdom" and not of his (Jesus') Kingdom. When the concept of having faith in Jesus became the heart of Christianity, the Gospel of God was side-stepped.

Finally, in their zeal for elevating the prestige and eminence of their prophet above all other prophets (and in turn elevating their own prestige), the Councils of Bishops introduced 'Creeds' and once and for all silenced the words of

---

[50] One of the major task of the Muslim scholars has been to categorize the reported sayings of the prophet Muhammad as authorized, not so authorized and otherwise.

[51] For further information on Islam read *The Concise Encyclopedia of Islam* by Cyril Glasse, Harper and Row, (1989).

their beloved prophet. The Creed made an honest messenger of God, into god.

When an easy way out is shown to the worshippers, they are more than willing to give up the hard one. Keeping the faith in Jesus was easier than keeping to his words, which demanded keeping the 'Law'. Adoration of lofty statues of Jesus, his Cross and the altar with candles became the symbol of faith. The true intentions of Jesus were completely overshadowed by elaborate pageantry and the solemnity of orthodox liturgy.

"Religious hypocrisy," writes Tom Harpur, "is far worse than the sins of harlots and tax collectors. Those who make a great show of their religiosity and piety go into the Kingdom of Heaven after those they consider sinners."

The Protestant Reformation rejected the idea of the priesthood standing between a Church-goer and his God. Protestants refuse to accept any external spiritual authority that is ultimate and created or dominated by men. The Holy Book became the sole authority. They also reject beliefs that imply the possibility of self-justification before God. They threw out the rituals of Transubstantion, the Mass and some other orthodox practices but held fast to the church elevated (not the Bible elevated), personality of Jesus (e.g. the Trinity).

Christians proudly say, quoting Roman 14:8, **"...we live for the Lord (Jesus)...we die for the Lord (Jesus)."** I wish, one day they would all say "We live for the Father (Alone) and we die for the Father (Alone)."

Muslims have been very careful to not make the same mistake. The Koran had explicitly and emphatically declared that Muhammad was a "slave of Allah," possessing no knowledge of what is going to happen tomorrow or thereafter. The concept of having any form of mediator is also negated in the Koran. Muslims have been warned that on the Day of Judgment all these intercessors will be of no avail and will deny having claimed any power of intercession. In Islam, the keys to the Kingdom of Heaven do not lie in the hands of the priests and prophets or the apostles and advocates. When God created man, none of them did intercede and so it shall be at the time of reckoning. An act of witnessing is often confused with an act of intervention.

But, in every society there are a few devious minds that want to line their own pockets by unethical means. For them, religion is a thriving business and customers are plentiful. Below are the last two paragraphs of the article from the newsletter quoted above:

> "Today we see that religion as an industry has become a flourishing source of income for unscrupulous saints and self appointed religious leaders among Christians as well as Muslims. Amongst Muslims tombs are built, offerings are made and prayers are said in order to win the interred's intercession on the Day of Judgement. Every year a fair is organized around their tombs and graves. All conceivable attractions are present to lure people and empty their purses. Games, Music and other entertainment for the pleasure seeking; trade and profit for the merchants; gambling facilities and even drugs. For the more pious devotees, story tellers relate the heroic deeds of their saints, recount their mystical powers and sing their praises. Religion has become a booming business.
>
> ...Worship of the Almighty alone has been replaced by worship of Syyedina Ali, Hussein and Khwaja Mu'eenuddin Chisti. If we Muslims want to escape the curse ... it is about time that we followed Allah's commandments, discard *Shirk*[52] and adopt *Tawheed* (Unity of God) in its purest form. (Extract from *The Many Shades of Shirk*)."

Recently an individual from the United States has claimed that there is a built-in mathematical code within the letters and words of the text of the Koran, based upon number

---

[52] *Shirk* means associating or ascribing equals to Allah. Shirk is considered as the greatest sin in Islam and regarded as unpardonable.

"nineteen". Upon closer scrutiny it is discovered that the claim is not based upon an explicit revelation but upon a surmise. There is no indication in the Koran, clear or otherwise, that the text has been coded. The claimant has added letters (e.g. 68:1) and deleted letters (e.g. 96:1-5), to the prevalent Arabic text to prove his theory. Furthermore, the individual claims himself to be a "messenger of God" receiving "commands" through Gabriel to make "announcements" from time to time.

There are also some books in the market written by Christian scholars making similar claims for the Bible and Jesus Christ on the basis of theomatics. These scholars argue that an interrelation of certain numbers prove that God wrote the Bible. Their numerical code is based upon numerical values of Hebrew and Greek alphabets. Jewish scholars have also made similar claims in the past. However, none of these claims are taken seriously.

DO YOU KNOW THIS PREACHER?

One day, some time in 1988, my wife and I watched a television program. Many of my readers may have seen this program and could bear me out. I did not take notes but the gist of it was as follows:

A preacher, who had very devotedly served Lord Jesus during his lifetime, was being interviewed. He was narrating his personal experience of a brief period when he was declared clinically dead. He informed the audience that he was led through a passage and presented before his God. He could not see Him but only hear His voice.

His God told him that he had not served *Him* during his lifetime, although he had the opportunity to do so. The preacher was a little puzzled and requested God to give him a second chance, so that he might serve Him with added devotion and efforts. The preacher then narrated that God instructed him to make sure that he would serve *Him.* He was revived by the doctors and had got the second chance to serve his God.

The preacher told the interviewer that he had served Jesus all his life, but since his God had instructed him to make sure that he serve Him, he wish to serve Lord Jesus, more vigorously than before.

My wife and I thought the poor preacher had not understood "the Message" of his True Lord, the Creator before who he was presented. Furthermore he had not even understood the message of his Jesus, who said to Satan:

> **"Begone, Satan! For it is written,**
> **'YOU SHALL WORSHIP THE LORD YOUR GOD, AND SERVE HIM ONLY."**
> Matthew 4:10

I wish the preacher would read this passage and understand "the Message" of Almighty God as it was supposed to be received. I wish the said preacher would take a moment to reflect as to why "God Jesus" would criticize him and tell the one, who has served "Lord Jesus" all his life, that he had not served *Him?*

I would be thankful if anyone who saw the program and knows the name of the preacher would communicate with me or convey this message to that preacher.

> **"Father forgive them,**
> **for they do not know what they are doing."**
> Luke 23:34

> **Say: "O men, the truth has come to you**
> **from your Lord.**
> **Whosoever is guided is guided only to his own gain,**
> **and whosoever goes stray, it is only to his own loss.**
> **I am not a guardian over you."**
> Koran 10:108

> "To hate truth as truth...
> is the same as to hate goodness
> for its own sake"
>
> Ethan Allen,
> *Reason the Only Oracle of Man,* 1794.

"Reason inspired by love of truth is the only eye with which man can see the spiritual heavens above us."

Chales E. Garman,
Letters, Lectures, Addresses, 1909.

...may the Lord show loving kindness and truth to you... (Amen)

2 Samuel 2:6

> ℂThe Byble in
> Englyshe, that is to saye the content of all the holy scrypture, bothe of ye olde and newe testament, truly translated after the veryte of the hebrue and Greke textes, by ye dylygente studye of dyuerse excellent learned men, expert in the forsayde tonges.
>
> ℂPrynted by Rychard Grafton & Edward Whitchurch.
>
> ℂum priuilegio ad imprimendum solum.
> 1 5 5 9.

☐   YES, I believe Jews, Christians and Muslims should rediscover their roots and the heavenly thread that links their Holy Books. It is time to transmute the strains of discord into harmony. Send me/us information on Special Propagation Discounts for ***Understanding the Bible.***

Name* _____

Address _____

Postal/Zip Code _____

Phone _____ Quantity _____ copies.**

*In case of non-profit organizations please mention income-tax exemption registration number or use your printed letter-head.

**In the multiples of twelve.

Mail to: **A.M. TRUST**
P.O. Box 82584
BURNABY, B.C.
Canada. V5C 5Z1
(604) 298-8803